The Verity Bargate Award New Plays 1986

RELEEVO by David Spencer
SMITH by Johnnie Quarrell
MADE IN SPAIN by Tony Grounds

Selected from over a hundred scripts by a panel of judges which included *Times* drama critic Irving Wardle and *Adrian Mole* creator Sue Townsend, *Releevo*, a first play by a previously unperformed author, was the outright winner of the third Verity Bargate Award, established specifically to encourage new writers.

Releevo, subsequently premiered at the Soho Poly Theatre in May 1987, looks with extraordinary authenticity and humanity at a dangerously disintegrating young working-class marriage. Also included in the volume are the two runners up: *Smith*, by Johnnie Quarrell, a hard-hitting play about race prejudice and prison corruption, and *Made in Spain* by Tony Grounds, a witty and satirical comedy about the joint plight of four suburban wives.

DAVID SPENCER was brought up in Halifax, West Yorkshire. His parents are Irish. *Releevo* in his first play. He has a degree in biology from Nottingham University, is 29 and lives in London.

JOHNNIE QUARRELL was born in Stepney in 1935. He is an ex-docker and steelfixer, and now works for a consortium bank in the City. He started writing plays in 1969 and has had his work read and performed at the Mermaid, Half Moon, Royal Court and Soho Poly theatres. His work for theatre includes *The Third and Final Round* (1984) and for the radio, *Steve and Eddie* (1986).

TONY GROUNDS was born in Ilford in 1957 and worked on the commodity markets before taking up drama teaching and playwriting. His plays include *Pillow Talk* and *The Irons* for the National Student Theatre Company and *Get Out of That, Then!* for the Lyric Theatre. He has written plays for his pupils at King Alfred School in North West London, including *The Play's the Thing*, performed at the Lyric Studio, and *Holiday in the Sun*. His play *The Kiss* was performed at the Swan Theatre Stratford as part of the R.S.C. Youth Festival sponsored by W.H. Smith. He is currently working on his first film commission. *Made in Spain* was first performed at the New End Theatre Hampstead in July 1987.

THE
VERITY BARGATE AWARD
NEW PLAYS 1986

edited by
BARRIE KEEFFE

RELEEVO
by David Spencer

SMITH
by Johnnie Quarrell

MADE IN SPAIN
by Tony Grounds

A Methuen Drama Paperback

METHUEN DRAMA

First published in Great Britain in 1987 by Methuen London Ltd

Releevo copyright © 1987 by David Spencer
Smith copyright © 1987 by Johnnie Quarell
Made in Spain copyright © 1987 by Tony Grounds

The authors have asserted their moral rights

ISBN 0 413 42120 1

A CIP catalogue record for this book is available at the British Library.

Typeset by Tek-Art Ltd, Croydon, Surrey
Transferred to digital printing 2003

The Verity Bargate Award

In 1969 Verity Bargate and Fred Proud set up the Soho Theatre Company in Soho. It moved to its present location in Riding House Street in 1971 where it became the Soho Poly Theatre. From this base Verity gave the first helping hand to hundreds of new writers by premiering their work. As Artistic Director she gained the theatre an international reputation for her work with new and developing writers and the one act play. Some of the writers whose early work she premiered were: Howard Brenton, Pam Gems, Gilly Fraser, Brian Clark, Tony Marchant, and myself.

This award was established after her death in 1981 to commemorate the remarkable contribution made by a woman of extraordinary instinct and drive in the field of new writing, and to carry on her work by the continuing encouragement of new playwrights.

Eligibility
The only restrictions on entries were that they should be new, unperformed plays and that they should be suitable for production at a small theatre such as the Soho Poly. The award comprises a cash prize and publication by Methuen London.

Selection
The one hundred and forty plays received were all read and reported on by professional readers. Many were read by more than one person. A short list of four plays was then drawn up by a committee consisting of Sue Dunderdale, Artistic Director of the Soho Poly, Patrick Cox, the Theatre's Administrator, and Tony Craze, writer-in-residence. The judges made their final selection from these four plays. All were given the same consideration regardless of style, content and form; quality and potential were the only guidelines.

Judges
The judges for the 1986 award were: Tony Craze, playwright and writer-in-residence at the Soho Poly; Carolyn Pickles, actress; Adrian Shergold, director; Sue Townsend, author and playwright; and Irving Wardle, drama critic of *The Times*. Sue Dunderdale, Artistic Director of the Soho Poly, and Nick Hern, drama editor of Methuen London, acted as moderators.

Awards
The judges nominated David Spencer's *Releevo* as the outright winner and recipient of the 1986 award but agreed that the two other plays in this volume merited publication.

Barrie Keeffe

Contents

RELEEVO

by David Spencer

For Quincy and Max

Characters

JULIE, middle twenties
STEVEN, her husband, late twenties
TOMMY, a neighbour, early thirties

There are various voices off. If the children are 'live effects' then they should be considered as players.

The action takes place in the front room and kitchen of a council house in West Yorkshire.

Scene One

Sunday, just before 7.00 p.m. November 1974.

JULIE *waits by the front-room window. Outside* KIDS *play. She pulls on her cigarette, slow and deep. Smoke funnels out through her nose and curls up around her hair. She checks her wristwatch. She pulls on her fag.*

Her suitcase is beside the stair-door. She takes a pull on her cigarette and stares at the suitcase. She rests the butt of her fag in an ashtray on the coffee table.

GIRL (*off*): Tred on a nick. Yer'll marry a brick. An' a snake 'ull cum t'yer weddin. (*Repeat. This has a low chant-like quality.*)

JULIE *checks her wristwatch time against the kitchen wall-clock. She lights a fag.*

JULIE: Wun o'clock. Wun o'bloody clock eh?

The wall-clock has stopped. Twenty-five past five. She climbs onto a chair and takes the clock off the wall. She dumps the spent batteries in the kitchen bin. A stew simmers on the kitchen cooker. She adds water from a kettle to the pan. She glides back to the front window.

Allus a gang ov 'em. (*Long pause.*) Same as midges.

Allow the young girl's chant to build through the above movement. Fade as the game action begins.

BOY (*off*): No wun chase Gigs. 'E's bin owta bounds. 'E's bin off estate.

JULIE: Gas lamps. Allus midges 'n' kids'. (JULIE *scratches her head.*) Got me thinkin on midges now.

BOY (*off*): Jimmy. Jimmy. Thorpey's there. Thorpey's be'ind Farrar's. Get Spanner. A've seen Thorpey.

JULIE: Bet young Duddy's glad a' that crop. Nitty Nora the bug explorer.

Poor lad. (*Pause.*) 'E looks like a refugee.

BOY (*off*): 'E's there. Ger'im. (*The sound of a scuffle as* THORPEY *makes a run for the post.*) 1.2.3.4.5.6.7.8.9.10. Releevo. (*The numbers are spoken as fast as possible, one running into the next.*) We've got Thorpey. We've got Thorpey.

JULIE: Kids round gas lamps. Midges round their 'eads.

BOY (*off*): Yew guard that post. D'yer 'ear me? Guard that post. If anywun gets Releevo yer dead.

JULIE: Tsk. B'sober Steven.

BOY (*off*): Just dunt let anywun touch it. That's all.

JULIE: Please be. Fer bloody wunce.

JULIE *walks to the kitchen. She is deep within herself. Her movements are resigned and mechanical. On the table is a rolling-pin and board, beside the board is a small brown bottle. She picks up the bottle and shakes two pills into her palm. She swills them down with a glass of water.*

JULIE *presses the pin against the board. After a few sharp rolls a white powder collects against the pin. She brushes the powder from the pin to her palm.*

JULIE *tips the powder from her palm into tips the powder from her palm into the stew. She watches as the powder sinks into the boil and lids the pan. She returns to the front room. She puts a record on: 'Stop in the Name of Love', by Diana Ross and the Supremes. (Substitute another Supremes number if it's not available.)*

JULIE *mimes into the Elvis Presley mirror for a few seconds. She leaves off and walks to the window. After about ten seconds she becomes bored and takes the record off. She goes into the kitchen. Relights her fag. She sees her pill container by the board. She lids it and pockets it. She checks the meal. She picks up an old tranny. It's tuned to the BBC Sunday chart rundown.*

We only hear the radio when it is at JULIE's *ear. Reception is poor (use Chartshow tape from November 1974, or snatches of neutral records: Stylistics; Elton John etc., one pre-seven time-check should be heard.)*

She walks into the front room and takes up a position by the window.

BOY (*off*): Mister. Mister. A'm stuck mister. Gee us an 'and mister.

JULIE *opens the window.*

STEVEN (*off*): 'Ang on lad. 'Ang on. A've got yer. Are yer reet?

JULIE: Steven. Yer dinna's ready. Leave the kids alone. (JULIE *closes the window.*)

Enter STEVEN, *via the side-door.*

STEVEN: Gud ev'nin.

STEVEN *goes into the toilet. He sings.*

Get into that kitchen an' rattle those pots 'n' pans . . .

JULIE: Wun o'clock yew sed Steven.

STEVEN (*sings*): Goody goody. Bow wow.

STEVEN *flushes the toilet. He comes out of the bathroom. He lopes towards* JULIE. JULIE *backs off and stands firm. He leans against the door and looks at* JULIE's *suitcase.*

JULIE: Yer drunk.

STEVEN: A'm not. A've 'ad a few jars. A'm not pissed.

JULIE: W'er've yer bin?

STEVEN: A've bin werkin. A tuk a few bottles round't shed.

JULIE: Wun o'clock's w'at yer sed.

STEVEN: No a dint. A sed a'd be back fer me dinna. An' a'm back fer it.

JULIE: W'er've yer bin all neet?

STEVEN: Luk luv. A wa upset. A'm sorry.

JULIE: Yew wer upset? 'Ow d'yer think a . . .?

STEVEN: Ohw cum on luv. A've sed a'm sorry. Gee us a kiss. Gow on luv.

JULIE: Yer sorry. Yer bloody stink.

STEVEN: A've got yer a presen' . . .

JULIE: Yer actin like nowt 'appened. An' it did. Steven a dunt want yer presen's. A wanna know w'er yew bin?

STEVEN: A went up club. A wa so smashed a . . .

JULIE: Not all day. An' all neet. A'm not stupid. Yew wer we that bloody cow? (*Pause. Quietly.*) Just tell me w're yew bin.

STEVEN (*shouts*): A've teld yer w'er a bin. (*Pause.*) So a've bin on't piss. It's n'bloody crime. Now a want me dinna. (*Pause.*) A got smashed in't club. After w'at . . . well w'at . . . w'at . . . A stayed at Sam Shaw's. (STEVEN *moves to the record-player.*) A've 'ad enuff.

JULIE: A'll get yew yer dinna. Yer can gee yer choc'lates t'yer fancy bit. A want nuthin from yew. Never. N'mor.

STEVEN *puts a record on: 'Mystery Train' by Elvis Presley. (If unavailable use an up-tempo Elvis, e.g. 'Hound Dog'). Crank the volume up.*

JULIE *slaps* STEVEN's *stew into a dish.* STEVEN *opens a bottle. He has another by his side. He drops his coat on the floor. He slurs along with the record.* JULIE *brings in the stew.*

D'yer 'afta 'ave that noise on?

STEVEN: It's the King of rock 'n' roll.

STEVEN *uses only his fork. He slurps the liquid from the dish.* JULIE *lifts his coat. She checks the pockets. She watches as* STEVEN *swigs his beer and then she carries his coat to the stair-bottom.*

Leave the bloody volume w'er it is.

She hangs up his coat. She tidies the records.

W'er's t'paper?

When the record finishes JULIE *takes it off.* STEVEN *is whistling and mumbling the theme from 'Mystery Train'.*

JULIE: There's summat a want ter say.

STEVEN *pigs the last of his stew. He gawps around the room. He swills down the last of his first bottle and wrenches open the second.* JULIE *flings the empty bottle into the bin.*

STEVEN: Temper.

JULIE: D'yer want mor?

STEVEN: A want the bloody paper.

JULIE *takes* STEVEN's *plate into the kitchen.*

STEVEN (*shouts*): W'ere've yew put it?

JULIE (*shouts*): A dunt know w'er it is.

STEVEN (*shouts*): W'er the bloody 'ell is it?

JULIE (*shouts*): It's under't cushion. On yer seat. (*Pause. She shouts.*) But ther's summat ter say. (JULIE *walks to the front room. She picks up the ashtray from the coffee-table. She takes up her position by the window.*) Steven. It wunt tek long. So put down't paper. They've shaved young Duddy's 'ead. (*Pause.*) Steven. Steven. Will yew bloody listen.

STEVEN: W'a? Yer?

JULIE: They've shaved young Duddy's 'ead. Poor sod'll 'av 'ad nits. (STEVEN *resumes his reading.*) No 'arm in 'avin 'em . . .

STEVEN: Only 'arm in breedin 'em. Aye. A know.

GIRL (*off*): A can see 'im. A can see 'im. Suts is there.

JULIE *lights a fag and scans outside.*

JULIE: Yer know ev'rythin yew dew.

Ev'rythin an' nowt. That's w'at yew know.

BOY (*off*): Guard that post.

JULIE: A'm gunna gow. (*Pause.*) A ampt unpacked me case.

GIRL (*off*): Dunt let 'im through. Dunt let 'im through.

JULIE: A dunt want ter gow.

GIRL (*off*): Spanner. Spanner. Ger'im Spanner.

Sounds of a scuffle. A cheer.

BOY: (*off*): Cum on Suts. Cum on.

JULIE: But a'd be a fool ter tek anymor. An' a'm not a fool.

BOY (*off*): Reeeee-lllll-eeeee-vvvvv-ooooo.

The sound of the free team escaping.

Wally. Yer daft bugger. Yer free. Run Wally. Run.

JULIE: Sutcliffe's lad's med post. They'll not see that lot now. Scot free. All ov 'em. (JULIE *turns to* STEVEN. *He's reading.*) A dunt know 'ow long a'll stay away. A'll just see 'ow a feel. Me mum's expectin me. (*Pause.*) A'm definitely gowin. (*Pause.*) If yew'd a bin early we might 'a talked. It might 'a bin different. A proper chance fer yew ter say yer wer sorry. (*Pause.* STEVEN's *paper falls to his lap.*) But yew bein late. An' actin like nowt's 'appened. It's med me mind up. Aye. This an' that.

She runs her hand across her left cheek. It stings. She looks across to the cupboard top. Her framed certificate is lying face down.

All that wer't bloody last straw. (*Pause.*) They've got young Sutcliffe already. Think on that time yer caught me owt back o'Hickey's. We wer playin Releevo then. A sed a'd gee yer a kiss if yer let me go. (*Pause.*) Yer took yer bloody kiss. Let me go. An' quick as a flash yer gripped me again (*Say the numbers as fast as possible.*) 1.2.3.4.5. 6.7.8.9.10. Releevo. (*Pause.*) Served yer right if yer remember. 'Cus Martin Challner got ter't post and got Releevo abowt two minutes after. A wa off like a shot. (*Pause.*) Yer only caught me't next time cus a wa bored. (STEVEN *snores.*) Well luv. Yer got yer kiss. (*Pause.*) An' now am gunna gow. That Mrs Hammond sed it wer a good idea. (STEVEN *snores.*) So that's w'at a'm doin. Steven. Steven. (*She moves to STEVEN and shakes him.*) Steven. Steven. Yer . . .

STEVEN (*drunken mumble*): Yeah. (*Pause.*) Freight train. Coming round the bend.

JULIE: Steven.

STEVEN: Yeah.

He waves JULIE away. He tries to resume his sleep. JULIE gives him a bitter look. She walks to her case.

JULIE: A'm gowin. (*Pause.* She puts her case down.*) Tommora Steven. Tommora.

JULIE tugs up the empty dish and storms into the kitchen. She lights her fag and walks to the front room. Her certificate is face down on the cupboard. She picks it up and takes a look.

Yer dint 'ear a werd. Did yer? W'en wer't last time yew listened ter me? A'm trying ter say . . . Get up Steven. Dunt fall asleep there. (JULIE *shakes him. He mumbles incoherently about Elvis Presley 'The King of rock 'n' roll.' She tries to pull him up by the arm. He shakes her off.*) Ger' up Steven. Ger'up. A'll leave yew there. Steven. Steven. Cum on.

GIRL (*off*): N'bdey's gunna chase yer. Yew've bin caught. Ev'rybodey knows. Yew've bin caught.

STEVEN: Lea' me alone.

After a few tries she pulls STEVEN to his feet.

A'm all reet 'ere.

GIRL (*off*): Yer might as well gee up. Yer a cheat.

JULIE (*motherly tone*): Cum on. Cum 'ere.

GIRL (*off*): Cheater. Cheater. Ev'rybodey knows.

STEVEN: A dunt know Julie. (*Pause.*) A'm pissed. (*Pause.*) I'll neva be n'good. W'at d'yer want? (STEVEN *makes a half-hearted attempt to cuddle JULIE.*)

JULIE: Stop pissin abowt.

STEVEN: A'm sorry, yer know. Abowt it all. A luv yer Julie. A luv yer. (*They get to the stair-door. JULIE props him against the wall whilst she opens the door.*) A luv yer. (*He slides down the wall.*)

JULIE: A believe yer. Thousands wunt. (*As he hits the floor JULIE opens the door.*) Ohw. Bloody 'ell. (JULIE *tries to drag him up the stairs but he's too heavy.*) Bloody 'ell. (*Long pause.*) Yew'd gow 'aywire if a left yew 'ere. (*She drags him back to the chair and gets him a glass of water.*) Yew need that fer the mornin. (*She quickly tidies around the house: ashtray, curtains, etc.*)

Lights gradually fade to black.

Gud neet.

She goes out of the stair-door and closes it.

Scene Two

Monday, mid-morning the next day. STEVEN sits in his chair. He doesn't move. His head is angled slightly to the right. JULIE backs through the stair-door. She drags the vacuum cleaner into the middle of the front room.

The sound of vacuum cleaner.

JULIE (*shouts*): Steven. D'yer want fish fingers? If yer 'ave fish fingers fer dinna a wunt 'ave ter gow owt. OK? So we'll 'ave fish fingers. A'll mek us a shepherd's pie for tea. (*Pause.*) It's first time yew've been 'ome fer ages. That spare room still needs decoratin. (*Pause.*) Move yer legs Steven. (*Pause.*) If yer Linda's gunna cum an' stay a'm not showin me sen up we a tip. (*Pause.*) Move yer legs will yer. Yew ampt ett owt. (*She snatches up the plate and switches off the vacuum. She shouts as though the vacuum is still on.*) Can yew . . . (*Realising she's shouting.*) 'ear me? (*Pause.*) A'll mek sum fresh tea. Yer can 'ave cereals instead. A dunt think cereals is a man's meal. If it stays fine there's allus that fence.

Once in the kitchen her bravado drops. Her movements and vocal tone are nervous. She shouts:

Yew promised me yer'd dew that fence. That dog a' White's uses our garden as a bloody bog.

JULIE *turns up the heat beneath the kettle. She slides the dishes into the sink. Her pill container is on the table. She unlids it and takes a long look. She watches as the kettle boils. It whistles.*

She makes two mugs of tea and carries them as far as the front-room door.

Meybe we cud g'fer a walk. If yer brighten up. Be nice that. (*She puts the tea down on the arm of* STEVEN's *chair.*) A'll just 'ave a fag n'all finish off. (*She picks up an ashtray and takes up her position by the window. She takes two blue baby-shoes from her pocket and examines them.*) Guess w'at a found? W'en a was tidyin in't bedroom . (*She holds the shoes out, expecting* STEVEN *to comment.*) They're them shoes yer Linda gee us. There's a few other kiddies' clothes tew. Most ov 'em are blue. (*Pause.*) Wunt a bin no gud if it 'ad a bin a girl. Still it were nice ov 'er. (*She pockets the shoes and takes a few nervy slurps of tea. She drags on her fag a few times.*) A think abowt w'at it wud'a

luked like. That's normal yer know. That Mrs Hammond sed so. (*Pause.*) Sometimes a've thought it wer still inside me. Yer know. Aye well. Yew wunt. Wud yer? But that Mrs Hammond. She sez it's normal. Drink yer tea luv. (*Pause.*) W'en a 'ear't kids. Bet yew think a'm bein morbid. (*Pause.*) W'en a 'ear 'em. Well morbid. (*Pause.*) W'en a 'ear 'em. Well a think . . . (*Pause.*) . . . A just think 'ow things might 'a bin different. (*Pause. She stubs out her fag.*) It just gows ter show. Wait till yer see w'at else a found. (*She looks around quickly. She takes the vacuum to the stair-bottom. She returns carrying a photo album.*) Most ov the pictures ov yew 'ave 'ad their 'eads cut off. A know it's not funny. A must 'a dun it after wun 'a ower rows. But there're sum nice ens. Oh my God. Mor a reminder than a memento. There. See. A told yer yer'd put on weight. Look. (*Pause.*) D'yer remember? It were ace. Anyroad. A thought so. Howarth. Yew an' me playin Charlotte an' w'atever. Yew in yer blazer. Yer dint 'ave a drink. (*Pause.*) Why d'yer drink? (*Pause.*) Yer more fun w'en yer dunt drink. (*Short pause.*) Luk. That's w'er yew got me this bangle. Meks a mark on me wrist but a still wear it. It's tew tight. See. Like bloody you. Too tight for anythin these days. Only 'ave ter kiss yer an yer run a mile. (*Pause.*) Oh Steven. W'en yew picked me up in yer arms a thought a wer't Queen. Only thing brighter then yer eyes wer yer blazer buttons. Why did yer ever put me down? Steven yew bastard. Dunt just sit there w'en a'm talking tew yer. Luk. Luk at it. Luk at the mark it's med on my bloody wrist.

She crosses the room and flops down in her chair. Gets comfy. She realises she's left her fags by STEVEN's *chair. She gets up and crosses the room to pick up the packet. She flops back in her chair. She fumbles a fag into her mouth, goes to light it and realises she's left her matches by the window.*

Oh bloody 'ell. (*Stands.*) Dunt worry Steven. A'm not blamin yew.

She retrieves the matches, flops into her chair and lights her fag. She throws her empty packet at the bin. She misses. She looks at the packet and then at the bin as if she might get up and bin the packet.

Bugger it. (*She takes a few drags and tries to get comfy in her chair. She glances at the packet.*) Bugger it.

She takes a few puffs and stares at the packet. Still staring at the packet she takes the fag from her mouth as if it has become suddenly distasteful.

A'm gunna gee 'em up. That'll surprise yer. Surprise the bloody world. Aye. Julie's geein up the fags.

She crosses the room and empties her ashtray into the bin. She picks up the packet and makes sure it's empty. She drops it in the bin.

And bugger yew an' all.

Blackout.

Scene Three

Monday, the same day, 8.00 p.m.

STEVEN *is in his chair. He doesn't move. His head is slumped to the right. This is the only change in his position.*

Light fades in.

The theme music from 'Coronation Street' just ending.

JULIE *walks to the TV and switches it off.*

The sound is very important in this scene. It is viewpointed in JULIE. *It is an attempt to portray her state of mind.*

KIDS (*voices over*): Dip dip dip. My blue ship. Sailin on the water like a cup an' saucer. Yew do not 'ave it. (*Repeat through dialogue. Build up the volume gradually.*)

JULIE: Yew must be ill. Yew've sat

threw't 'Street' we'out a werd. (*Pause.*) Pass us paper Steven. (*Pause.*) Gow on. Please luv. All reet. A'll get it me sen. (*She takes the paper from* STEVEN'*s lap.*) There'll be nowt on. (*Pause.*) There. See. Nowt on. A dunt know why we bother we't thing. Bloody doc-re-mentries. (*She goes to the kitchen.*)

Sound levels out. She shouts:

Pie'll be ready soon. D'yer want sum? (*She walks to the connecting door.*) 'Ave sum Steven. A'll dew toms we it. It smells luvly. All reet then. Yew dunt want n'pie. We'll 'ave it later. (*Pause.*) Maybe yer'd like a drink. A cud gow ter Morris's. It'll still be open. A cud get sum cigs tew. Yer sayin yer dunt want n' beer? (*Pause.*) Maybe later? W'en yew've 'ad yer dinna? (*Pause.*) Yer'd like a cushion though? (JULIE *tries to prop a cushion behind* STEVEN'*s head.*) Tsk. Neva mind.

BOY (*off*): Ova there. Yer on't 'idin side.

At the same time as the sound, JULIE *goes to the window. The* KIDS *are getting to her. She has a headache.*

If we catch yer we'll bring yer ter't post. If wun a yer men touches it an' shouts Releevo yer free. (*Short pause. Resume the rhyme/chant.*)

KIDS (*off*): Dip dip dip (*etc.*)

JULIE *hesitates. She does not draw back the curtain to look.*

JULIE: Wunce now an' again. It'd be all reet. But it's ev'ry bloody neet. A'm gunna mek sum tea. Yew'll 'ave sum if a mek it.

She goes to the kitchen. She puts the kettle on. Her headache is worse. She taps the pill container on the table but does not take one. She leaves the container on the table. She goes to the front room and flops in her chair.

KIDS (*off. Dipping out ends*): Yeaaaaa 'oooraaaaay. Now five 'undred in fives an' n'bloody lukin. (*As the* KIDS *run off the murmur drops.*) Five. Ten.

Fifteen. Twenty . . . (*Up to 100 and begin again.*) Five. Ten. (*Etc. Keep the chant forceful and rhythmic.*)

JULIE *tolerates the count for about five seconds.*

JULIE: It's like they're in't bloody room.

She searches through the records and puts on 'Band of Gold' by Frieda Payne. (If this is not available use a Supremes number.)

The combination of the noise of the record and the noise of the kids causes JULIE *physical pain. She pushes up the volume of the record. She mimes into the 'Elvis' mirror.*

KIDS (*off*): Five. Ten. (*Etc. The sound rises to drown the song.*)

JULIE *pushes up the volume. She is in pain.*

The sound of the KIDS *rises to drown the song.*

JULIE *pushes up the volume of the song.*

The sound of the count rises.

A neighbour knocks on the wall; knocks hard.

JULIE: All reet. A 'ear yer. A 'ear yer.

The neighbour knocks on the wall.

JULIE: It's them kids yer . . . (*She switches off the record.*)

The count is still loud and forceful. (It should be in the last one hundred now.)

The kettle starts to whistle.

JULIE *runs to the kitchen. She turns the gas off beneath the kettle. She swills two pills with a glass of water.*

The count ends.

KIDS (*off*): Oooooooowwwwraaay. Get gone. Cumin. Ready or not. Cumin. Ready or not. (*Keep this chant forceful and rhythmic.*)

JULIE *runs to the front room and*

flings open the window.

All noise stops instantly.

JULIE (*shouts*): Yer can all bugger off. Ger down yor own end. (*Pause. Double-takes. She can only see* JIMMY. *Shouts.*) Go on. All a yer. Bugger off down yer own end.

BOY (*off*): But missus. A only live tew doors away.

JULIE: If a've t'tell yer dad yew'll catch a leatherin. Me 'usband's not well. A dunt want nun a yer lip. (*Pause.*) Yer can tek rest ov 'em we yer.

BOY (*off*): But missus. A'm on me own.

JULIE: Aye. And rest are brob'ly laykin be'ind't 'edge.

BOY (*off*): A'm on me own. Yer . . .

JULIE (*shouts*): A mean it. N'mor lip. Or a'll be round yer 'ouse. (*She slams the window.*)

Blackout.

Scene Four

March 1974. Early evening.

JULIE *is in the kitchen. She's preparing food. She's dressed in a nylon housecoat. On her feet she has Mickey Mouse slippers.* STEVEN *enters via the side-door. He's carrying his anorak. In the pockets are a couple of travel brochures and a copy of Motorcycle News. Stuffed into his jeans' pocket is a wing mirror. He's polishing a metal cylinder.*

JULIE: Steven? Steven luv? That yew?

STEVEN: We're gunna be rich. Rich.

JULIE: Steven?

STEVEN (*to the tune of 'Jailhouse Rock'*): Der down. Der down. Warden threw a party at the county jail. Prison band was there. They began to wail.

JULIE: Give cat's a chance.

STEVEN (*imitates Elvis's movements; sings:*) Ev'rybedy in't whole cell block.

Was dancin to the 'Jailhouse Rock'.

JULIE: Yer early.

STEVEN: We finished early. So a went ter town. Got sum things. A 'ad a swift jar. An' a've cum 'ome.

JULIE: Steven. Dunt bring that mess in 'ere.

STEVEN: Nay. That mess is the last bit in a jigsaw worth five-'undred quid.

JULIE: Steven. Put sum newspaper down. An' pur'it on't floor.

STEVEN *hangs his coat on the chair-back. He takes the brochures from his pocket. He put them on the seat of the chair and rests the cylinder on them.*

STEVEN: Compromise. Cum 'ere me Pink Lady.

JULIE: A'up Steven. Yer in yer second child'ood.

STEVEN (*sings*): Love me tender. Love me true. All my dreams fulfil. (*As he sings he snakes his arms around her in such a way as to avoid touching her with his oily hands.*) Oh my darling I love you. And I always will. (*They kiss.*)
As they kiss the wing-mirror sticks into JULIE.

JULIE: Owwch! (STEVEN *fishes the mirror from his pocket and puts it on the cupboard behind* JULIE.) Yew'll get mess ev'ryw'ere. (*They kiss again.*) Now w'at wer yew on abowt?

STEVEN *takes his copy of Motorcycle News and spreads it on the kitchen table.*

STEVEN: Cum an' 'ave a luk at this.

JULIE: A can't Steven. A'll spoil't dinna.

STEVEN: Cum on.

JULIE: Yew read owt. Unless it's pictures.

STEVEN: 1958 BSA 500, single cylinder Gold Star. Newly renovated. £500 or nearest offer.

JULIE: Dunt be soft. We can't afford £500.

STEVEN: A'm not buyin one, woman. A'm sellin.

JULIE: A know Steven. A know. A little joke.

STEVEN: Ohwer. A'm sorry luv. A'm a bit excited.

JULIE: So yer shud be. D'yer reckon yew'll get that much?

STEVEN: Bit more. Mine's as old. But a've modernised electrics . . .

JULIE: Steven . . .

STEVEN: That means a can sell ter either a rider or a collector. We them new brakes. An' a slight rebore a'll . . .

JULIE: Steven . . .

STEVEN: W'at a'm sayin is. Yes luv. At least £500.

JULIE: Tek bread in't front room. (STEVEN *picks up the bread.*) An't knives an' forks. (*He picks those up and goes into the other room.*)

STEVEN (*shouts*): A went ter look at sum 'olidays. A really wanted ter g'tew Memphis. See't King. Yer know.

JULIE (*shouts*):King oow?

STEVEN (*shouts*): Elvis.

JULIE (*shouts*): Ohw. That king. Well. Go on.

STEVEN (*shouts*): Well. It wer t'much. But a got sum others. Spain n'that.

JULIE (*shouts*): Other w'ats?

STEVEN (*shouts*): Brochures.

JULIE (*shouts*): Yew've got sum brochures? W'er a'they?

STEVEN (*shouts*): They're on't chair. Under't 'ead.

JULIE (*shouts*): W'at 'ead?

STEVEN (*shouts*): Bloody cylinder 'ead.

JULIE (*shouts*): Owh Steven. They're all cuva'd in oil. (*Pause.*) A'd a liked ter luk at them.

STEVEN: A'll get sum tommora.

JULIE *hands* STEVEN *food.*

JULIE: W'at yer doin Steven?

STEVEN: Eh?

JULIE: Use yer knife.

STEVEN: Nay lass. Elvis eats like this.

JULIE: Ow d'yew know that?

STEVEN: A've seen in them films. Americans allus eat we their forks. Elvis is American. In't 'e?

JULIE: Meybe. But yer can't eat peas we a fork.

STEVEN *pretends to fire two guns. He imitates John Wayne.*

STEVEN: Nope. Butta a man's gotta chew. Ow a man's gotta chew. (*He laughs.*) D'yer ger it?

JULIE: Yer daft bugger. (*Short silence.*) Be nice ter 'ave an 'oliday.

STEVEN: A used ter luv chips at seaside.

JULIE: There's nowt wrong we them chips.

STEVEN: Aye. A know, luv. A wa just sayin. A used t'luv chips at seaside. Yer know. W'en yer lips were all salty from't sea. Ahw. It wer great.

JULIE: D'yer want sum salt on 'em?

STEVEN: There's nowt wrong we't chips. (*He eats a forkful.*) See. Great chips. (*Pause.*) A ett sum in me granny's mini once. On't Scarburra front. It wer only chips. But a remember it as though it wer chicken an' chips. It wer . . .

JULIE: Luk luv. If a'd a known we wer cumin in ter money a'd a got steaks.

STEVEN: Luv. There's nowt wrong we fish fingers. Or't chips. A'm trying ter tell yer summat. (*Pause.*) It wer cus a wer 'ungry them chips tasted ser gud.

JULIE: If yer not 'ungry. Leave 'em.

STEVEN: We allus went in't same chippy. Me mum'd cum. But me dad stayed 'ome. 'E'd be werkin in't yard. (*Pause.*) Garret's. That wer't name't chippy. Garret's. There wer a bloke there. Dennis. 'E gee me a ride on 'is bike.

JULIE (*imitates a violinist*): Der der der da der der der.

STEVEN: Dunt tek piss luv. (*Pause.*) Me mum wer shittin bricks. It wer a Triumph. A collector's piece be now. (*Pause.*) We went all round Scarburra Bay. A'd one o' them small peaked plastic 'elmets. An' a T-shirt . . .

JULIE: Eat yer tea Steven. It'll gow cold.

STEVEN: A wa dead scared. A clung tew 'im. Buried me 'ead in his back. Then a'd a funny thought fer a nipper. 'A either fall off. Or a dunt.' Ev'rythin wer faster'n wind. It wer real. (*Pause.*) A saw 'em kissin once. Me mum 'n' Dennis. She used ter get me an' our Linda ter call 'im Uncle Dennis. (*Pause.*) It wer't first bike a ever 'ad a go on.

JULIE: Well. They'll be more now.

STEVEN: Aye. Did a tell yer? A'm gunna call it Jubilee Bikes. Part after't road. Jubilee Road. An' part after yew.

JULIE: Ohwer yer? Great idea.

STEVEN: A wa gunna call it Flamin Star Bikes. After that Elvis cowboy film.

JULIE: Aye?

STEVEN: Yeah. But yer know w'at they're like round 'ere. It'd be flamin this an' flamin that if a wer ter call it flamin anythin. Good eh? (JULIE *takes the things into the kitchen. He shouts:*) It wunt be enuff on its own. But we w'at we've saved. An' we't wages an' all. A'll get a loan. We'll be in bis'ness.

JULIE *lights a fag and goes into the front room.* STEVEN *gives her 'the look.'*

JULIE: It's me first t'day.

STEVEN: Yeah. A believe yer.

JULIE: 'Onest. A like one w'en a finished me dinna.

STEVEN: A wish yer wunt.

JULIE: So do I.

STEVEN: A wa just abowt ter gee yer a big snog.

JULIE (*stubs out the fag*): Well a'd better be a good girl an' brush me teeth.

STEVEN *follows her.* JULIE *comes out of the bathroom brushing her teeth.* STEVEN's *leaning against the door.*

STEVEN: 'Ave yer eva dun it in't bath?

JULIE: Yer w'at?

STEVEN: It. Yer know. In't bath.

JULIE: Luv. A can count on wun finger't times a've dun it we'owt yew.

STEVEN: Yer mean yer 'ave dun it in't bath?

JULIE: No. A mean there wer only that one time we Peter. Then yew. Anyroad. W'at d'yer want ter dew it in't bath for?

STEVEN: Because. If yer dew it in't bath. It can't be dirty. Bum. Bum.

JULIE: Luv. We're married. It's not dirty anyway.

Lights down.

Scene Five

Sunday, late evening, 14 May 1974.

JULIE's *at the front-room window. It's early evening. She pulls on a fag and marches to the side-door.* STEVEN *lets himself in. He's carrying two large carrier bags.*

STEVEN: 'Ello luv.

JULIE: Dunt 'ello luv me. W'er've yer bin till this time?

STEVEN: A've bin ter't game. A've got yer a presen'. (*He pulls two garden gnomes out of one bag and puts them on the kitchen table.*) W'at d'yer reckon? (*Pause.*) It wer great. W'at a game. Dixie got wun a them concrete balls off top ov a gatepost. 'E carried it fer miles. Kensington tew Victoria. Laugh? A nearly shit me sen.

JULIE: W'at wer yer doin?

STEVEN: Yer know them sun tables yer allus on abowt. A tried t'get wun a them in a taxi. They've 'em outside all't pubs. Martini all ova't brolley. Bloody cabbie shit a 'orse. Shud 'a 'erd im. 'No way John. Not in 'ere mate.'

JULIE: W'ere've yew bin since Friday? It's bloody Sunday.

STEVEN: Anyroads. Yew'll 'ave ter dew we gnomes. A've summat else. (*He pulls two teatowels from the bag. One has 'London' on it.*) Luk. Nice in't they?

JULIE: Lunden. W'at yer bin dewin in Lunden?

STEVEN: Dint Tommy tell yer?

JULIE: Aye. He told me. Sat'dey dinna. Be then a'd waited most'a Fridey. A thought yew'd be back last neet.

STEVEN: Ahw. Luv.

JULIE: It's not bloody funny. A wa sure summat'd 'appened t'yer. A wa gunna call't police. A only went ter Sheila's fer a cig. She sed Tommy'd sed summat abowt yew an' sum game. W'at did yer bugger off we'owt tellin' me fer?

STEVEN: A tried ter get a message tew yer. Yew were at our Linda's. A saw Tommy an' told 'im.

JULIE: Why dint yer gee 'im a note?

STEVEN: Well er. A wa in a rush. A panicked. Yer know. (*Pause.*) A wer up an' down like a blue-arsed fly. (*He digs into the other bag and pulls out a*

Elvis Presley mirror.) Great eh?

JULIE: Yer allus owt. Or werkin. Weekend's only chance a've ter see yer.

STEVEN: A cun't wait n'longer. Tony an't lads wer ready fer 't off. A'd ter gow there 'n' then. Or gee it a miss.

JULIE: Tony?

STEVEN: Aye. Tony. 'E'd a spare ticket fer't game.

JULIE: W'at bloody game?

STEVEN: Bloody Rugby League Challenge Cup. A might be on't telly. A great match. And best is a've seld't bike.

JULIE: Yer sold it?

STEVEN: Aye.

JULIE: That's great. (*Pause.*) Yer ampt spent it 'ave yer?

STEVEN *pulls an account book from his pocket.*

STEVEN: £525's w'at a got. A've £503 left. We 'owt me labour a've med abowt £300 clear. We're in bis'ness. (*Pause.*) Anyroads luv. W'at d'yer think tew yer presen's?

JULIE: They're more fer't 'ouse then fer me. (*Pause.*) Yew ampt spent it. 'Ave yer?

STEVEN: Nooh. (STEVEN *pulls a bottle of wine from the bag.*) Stylish eh? Yew sit down. A'll pour.

JULIE *skips to the front room, bounces into her chair.* STEVEN *pulls two tea mugs from the cupboard. He pops the wine and the mugs proudly onto an old tin tray. He waltzes toward the front room. He shouts:*

A'm still laughin. Yer shud'a seen Dixie an' their kid. Them 'umpin that bloody great ball. They'd ter rest ev'ry ten yards. (*Pause.*) There yew are.

JULIE: Ohw Steven. We've got glasses yer know.

STEVEN: Stop fussin an' ger'it down yer.

A've summat ter tell yer. (*Pause.*) A'm goin in ter bis'ness we Tony. (*Pause.*) Now wait till yer 'ear w'at a've ter say afore yer start. A've seld wun bike. A can dew it again. But a want a quicker return. Tony knows the body-sprayin bis'ness like back ov 'is 'and. E needs a bit a capital. We us both werkin partners we'll 'ave't thing singin in a year.

JULIE: But a thought yew . . .

STEVEN: A've sum mor. (*Pause.*) We'll call it Jubilee Repairs. A'll be able ter dew bikes on't side. We stand ter mek a fair bit.

JULIE: But Steven. (*Pause.*) A just want yer ter be 'appy. Bikes 'as allus bin yer thing. Capital? Quick return? It all means nowt ter me.

STEVEN: Luk luv. It's only bis'ness talk. Yer dunt need ter understand it. Yer only need ter trust me. (*Pause.*) A was. A am. In ter bikes. A wunt be givin 'em up. All a'll be geein up is this.

JULIE: A like me little 'ouse. (*She lights a fag.*)

STEVEN: Luv. It all means mor money. Mor quickly. That means a 'ouse ov us own. W'at we want. There's nowt ter be scared ov. (*Pause.*) A'm 'andin in me cards at Macs.

JULIE: W'at?

STEVEN: Dun't worry. Not straight off. A'm waitin till we get goin. Then it's Jubilee Repairs. 'Ere we cum. N'more bloody yes red cap sir. No green cap sir. Bloody Adolf Hitler fer a charge 'and. Like bloody school. Puttin yer 'and up ter g'fer a piss. A'll be me own man now.

JULIE: 'Eld on luv. It's a job.

STEVEN: Aye. It's a job. Fer three days a week w'en it suits 'em. A bloody ape cud dew it. A wanna be me own boss. (*Pause.*) A'm not sayin yew gee up yours. It's yer bit a spend. But luv. It's the lot. Things yer want. 'Ouse. Bis'ness . . .

JULIE: Family . . .

STEVEN: A've this for yer.

He goes to the kitchen and comes back with a carrier. He pulls out an electric wall clock.

It runs on batt'ries. Better'n them wind-up things. New clock fer new times eh?

JULIE: Steven?

STEVEN: It wunt expensive. A wun it.

JULIE: 'Ow?

STEVEN: A wer playin't machines. A wun it. Su there yew are. We went ter Soho. Bloody 'ell lass. Yer shud'a seen summat things there.

He puts the clock on the coffee-table. He dips into the bags and pulls out a bright red nightie. It's made of a flimsy rayon.

And fer yew.

JULIE: Steven.

STEVEN: D'yew like it? It's fer yew.

JULIE: Nay luv. It's fer yew.

STEVEN: It's fer both ov us.

JULIE: Aye 'appen.

STEVEN pours them both more wine. He sits in his chair. JULIE holds the nightie against herself. She goes to the corner of the room and turns off the light.

Lights out.

STEVEN: Hey?

JULIE: Power cut. Shall we light a candle?

Scene Six

Monday, about 8.00 p.m., 3 June 1974.

STEVEN's *in the kitchen hunting out some beers.* TOMMY's *sat in* JULIE's *chair. Beside him is an empty beer can. On the coffee-table, two empty cans,* beside STEVEN's *chair an empty can and three account ledgers.*

STEVEN *locates a couple of cans and four small bottles.*

TOMMY (*shouts*): Well Steven. We know oow put the cunt in Scunthorpe.

STEVEN (*shouts*): Yer w'at Tommy?

TOMMY (*shouts*): Oow put the cunt in Scunthorpe?

STEVEN (*shouts*): A dunt fuckin know.

TOMMY (*shouts*): Nypro yer wazock.

STEVEN *puts the beers on a tray and carries them in.*

(*Shouts.*) That Flixburra thing. Yer know. Chemical werks w'at blew up. It's still burnin. Twen'y-four 'ours all teld. There's ova forty fire engines there. Still can't put the bugger owt.

STEVEN: Get that down yer. (*He puts the tray down on the coffee-table and hands* TOMMY *a beer.*) 'Ave the Russians still got Keegan?

TOMMY: Ah Steven. There's twen'y-nine men dead.

STEVEN: 'Ave the Russians let 'im go?

TOMMY: 'E's in Belgrade.

STEVEN: Yer? So w'at?

TOMMY: That's in Yew-go-slavia.

STEVEN: Yew-go-slavia. Russia. It's all 't same. We want 'im fit fer Wensdey. Me prediction's England three — Yew-go-slavia nil.

TOMMY: That's 'ow it all 'appened. Dozey gets oow run't England tour din't reckon on't 'ours time difference between Bulgaria and Yew-go-slavia. W'en't lads got ter't airport there wer n'bdey ther ter meet 'em. Su they got pissed up an' started prattin abowt.

STEVEN (*imitates a Chinese voice*): Ah so Master Po. Velly sow-we. Yew no piss about in 'onerable Communist country. We make earrings from yer bollacks. Bastards. Sulkin. England one — Bulgaria nil. Frankie Worthington

the scorer. A Huddersfield boy.
(*Pause.*) W'ere's our Julie?

Short silence.

TOMMY: Worthington plays fer Leicester
City. That's w'ere them Pakies are on
strike. Moss Evans' lot. Transport an'
General.

STEVEN: There's 'undreds o'the buggers
in Leicester. Mor than Bradford.

TOMMY: They say there's 'undreds up
Gibbet Road. A 'ardly ever see one.
Anyroads. It's about pay and
conditions. Not whether they're
wogs or not.

STEVEN: Aye. But a'm a bis'ness man
now. (*Pause.*) Ave a drink yer cunt.
A'm not bein serious.

TOMMY *opens his can, sips.* STEVEN
necks his can and gets a bottle.

TOMMY: Ow's it gowin anyroads?

STEVEN: Werks, all reet. (*Pause.*) Yer
know me. A can werk. Tony's a
straight enuff grafter tew. When yer
kick off it's ova'eads. Initial lay-owts.
That's w'at capital's all abowt. Plen'y a
money around. But it's n' quicker in
yer 'and then owt. (*Pause.*) Say sumwun
leaves us a respray. A lot a time their
insurance wunt pay. It's this betterment
shite. (*Pause.*) Sup up. That means
we've made their car better'n it wer
before. So't insurance'ull not pay't full
cost. Or't VAT. So w'en Joe Bloggs
cums and sez, 'Sorry can't pay,' we're
snookered.

TOMMY: Why dunt yer just keep their
car. Or 'it 'em on't 'ead we a wrench?

STEVEN: Tint that simple. VAT's
changed ev'rythin. Yer can't just 'it
people on't 'ead anymor.

TOMMY: Aye but yer cud keep their car.

STEVEN: We get a lot a jobs cash in't
'and. It's bread an' butter. Su we've ter
keep people 'appy. Till we build up.
Sumtimes a reckon we need an
accountant. Tony sez we'd 'ave ter go

straight if we'd an accountant.

TOMMY: Bollacks. That's w'at them
buggers are fer. There all as bent as
nine-bob notes. (*Pause.*) W'ats your
Julie say abowt it bein up in't air?

STEVEN: Up in't air? Fuck it Tommy.
A'm not bloody Poulson. It's a bit 'ere
an' a bit there. Our Julie sez nowt. Cus
she knows nowt. As long as she's her
keep she's laughin. (*Pause.*) Dunt look
at me like that. A'm doin w'at a shud.
A'm organisin this pension thing.
That's another set a bloody forms.
'Ere Tommy sup up. Yer sat there
like (*High pitched voice:*) 'mine's 'alf
a lagar an' lime.' (TOMMY *finishes his
can and takes a bottle from* STEVEN.)
Yew'll be on ter mortgages next. As
bad as't lass.

TOMMY: If yew'd an accountant yer . . .

STEVEN: D'yew know anywun we an
accountant? Do yer? (*Pause.*) W'at did
yer 'ave fer Satdey's card?

TOMMY: Nowt much. Fleetin Glance in't
Nightingale Stakes. Only did that cus
it wer on *Grandstand*. A wun a couple
a quid each way.

STEVEN: A'd Shepherds' Delight in that
un. Shuda know. Red bloody sky at
night. Fuck me. It came in fifth. This
is water this. There's mor clowt in a
wine gum.

TOMMY: Yer puttin em away.

STEVEN: W'ere's our Julie? It's dark at
nine. A wanna be owt be then. Get
sum proper pop down me neck.

TOMMY: We're off ter Spain. August
Bank. We're puttin't kids we me mam.
It'll be real. Just me an' our Sheila.

STEVEN: This stuff goes straight ter't
piss bag.

TOMMY: Are yew gettin away?

STEVEN: A fuckin 'ope so. If she gets
back. A wa thinkin Ex-Service for a
game a snooker.

TOMMY: A mean fer't wakes week. Wer

goin ter Spain.

STEVEN: That's all reet. It'll cost yer a bomb though. Kids an' all.

TOMMY: W'er are yer? A teld yer. Wer puttin't kids we me mam.

STEVEN: 'Oliday? All a dew is werk an' piss. A like piss but am bored we it. It's only thing w'at puts a bit a space between me an' werk. A never fuckin relax, me. (*Pause.*) Healy's sayin 'e's gunna put tax up next budget. Fuck knows w'at'll 'appen if Wilson puts us in't Common Market. Another tax. It's like that bloody decimalisation. A right con that wer. Our Julie's owt werkin fer 'er bit a spend. We've bloody decoratin ter dew. 'Olidays? Fuck me. 'Ad soon as go on't piss fer a week.

STEVEN *heads to the toilet.*

TOMMY: Steady on Steve. It in't that bad. (*He shouts when* STEVEN *gets to the bog.*) A wa in tew minds whether ter vote Labour. W'en Wilson said 'e wer gunna put ev'rywun back in werk a shit me sen. (*Pause.*) Three-day week. A luved it. Same money gee or tek a few quid. A wa laughin boy. A'd a left miners an' that lot w'er they wer. Not that a reckon they dint deserve more dosh. A just dint gee a toss.

The toilet flushes.

Ev'ry time't power went, me an our lass went straight ter bed. A'd a packet a Jaffa Cakes wun neet. It wer me first ever candle-lit meal except fer a curry. Me an' our Sheila. Never talked su much in years. A tell yer. If a'd finished HP an't telly wer mine a'd put me fuckin foot straight through it.

STEVEN *enters the front room.*

Present company excepted. A can't understand all this ova'time. Ova'time fer w'at? A wanna job w'at pays.

STEVEN (*opens last bottle*): A wunt

know w'at a want. Me bis'ness. Our Julie. (*Pause.*) Listen ter this. The man at 'is best. A dunt know why that Priscilla left 'im. Fuck knows w'er she'll end up.

He plays 'I've Got a Thing About You Baby' by Elvis Presley. (Release date Feb. 1974.) Alternatively an Elvis love song.

Short silence.

TOMMY: Paisley wer on't news. E . . .

STEVEN: Tommy. Fer fuck's sake. Yer soundin like *The World This Weekend.* Yer can tell mor from Mike Yarwood.

Short silence.

JULIE *enters via the side-door.*
STEVEN *turns the volume down; finishes his beer.*

JULIE: Steven? Steven?

JULIE *enters the room.* TOMMY *stands.*

TOMMY: 'Ello luv.

JULIE: Hiya Tommy. Are yer all reet?

TOMMY: Aye. (*Pause.*) Ower Sheila sez yew've ter cum round an' see 'er.

JULIE: That's nice. A will Tommy. Mec us sum tea Steven luv. (*She notices the beer bottles. Pause.*) There wer 'ell ter pay we't extra loadin. A dunt know oow buys all them biscuits. A can't eat 'em in this weather.

STEVEN (*to* TOMMY): Sit down. (TOMMY *sits.*) We're off owt. Yew'll ave'ter mek yer own tea.

JULIE: Oh Steven. Dunt be mean in frunt a Tommy. A wanna talk ter yer.

TOMMY (*stands*): We can 'ang abowt. (*To* STEVEN.) A cud pop 'ome. A'll be back in ten minutes.

JULIE: Please Steven. It's not as though yer thirsty.

STEVEN: Why wer yer late? Yer wern't packin all this time.

JULIE: A teld yer Steven. (*She mouths 'Cum on, cum on' and gestures toward*

the kitchen. TOMMY *does not notice.)*
'Ad ter gow ter Dr Walsh's surgery.
Leave them Tommy luv. A'll ger'em
w'en yer gone.

TOMMY: A 'ope yer not ill luv.

JULIE: Well it's serious. But am not ill. A
mainly went ter see abowt me tablets.
'E sez a shud cum off 'em soon.

STEVEN: Abowt bloody time.

JULIE: A can see a've ter mek me own
tea. *(To* TOMMY.*)* Din't 'e say nowt
tew yer?

TOMMY: 'E sed lots luv. 'E never
stopped talkin abowt yer.

STEVEN: Yer like a pair ov hens.

JULIE: It's funny yer shud say that.
They 'ad radio on at werk. Abowt that
Flixburra thing. One bloke sed most
ov 'is 'ouse wer blown up.'E'd a dozen
eggs on 'is pantry shelf. Not one wer
cracked.

TOMMY: They sed there wer twenty-nine
men dead.

JULIE: It's terrible in't it?

STEVEN: They sed that abowt Werld
War I. Terrible in't it? Werld War II
still 'appened.

JULIE: W'at yew on abowt?

STEVEN: Just cus a thing's terrible dunt
mean it wunt 'appen agen.

TOMMY: Aye aye misery guts.

STEVEN: It meks sense.

TOMMY: Aye. But a dunt see w'at kind a
sense.

STEVEN: Mec sum tea.

JULIE: A'm gunna do.

STEVEN: We're off for a game a snooker.

JULIE: Yew look like yew've played
a fair bit a snooker already.

STEVEN: Am goin owt. A ampt bin owt
all weekend.

TOMMY: Ahem.

JULIE: Yew wer owt Sat'dey. An'

Sundey. A cud smell it w'en yew cum
in.

STEVEN: That wer a couple we Tony
after werk.

TOMMY: A'd luv a cup a tea. A cud mek
wun if yer like.

JULIE: There yer are. Yew've embarrassed
Tommy.

STEVEN: Ohw. Mek sum tea if yer
'ave ter. We can wait a few minutes.

TOMMY: Yer cud cum up club. A'll get
ower Sheila.

JULIE: No Tommy. No need. *(Pause.)*
A'll see 'im w'en 'E gets back.

STEVEN: 'E's got a name.

JULIE: 'E's half sloshed.

JULIE *storms off to make tea.*

TOMMY: W'at's up we yer man? She's
bin ter't docters.

STEVEN: Mind yer own fuckin bis'ness.

TOMMY: A dint want ter see yer rowin.

Short silence.

STEVEN: Ferget it Tommy. *(Pause.)*
Nowts up we 'er. A dint want ter tell
yer w'en a'd bin drinkin. W'at a mean
is. A wanted ter tell yer. But w'en a'wa
sober. *(Pause.)* A'm gunna be a daddy.

Lights down.

Scene Seven

Friday, about 8.00 p.m., October 1974.

STEVEN *is in his chair. In his lap is an
account book. It's open. He stares at it
and pokes at the page with a pen. There
are two more account books lying open
on the floor. Beside them are two empty
beer bottles. On the arm of* STEVEN's
*chair is a half-full bottle. From time to
time he pulls on it.*

JULIE *leans against the back of her
chair. She is clearly pregnant.*

JULIE: Yer livin in a dream world
Steven. Yer dunt know w'at's goin on.

N'bloody wonder Tony gor'away we w'at 'e did. (*Pause.*) Luk luv. Yer either drunk, gettin drunk, or soberin up. A ampt seen yer sober fer't last six months. (*Pause.*) Yew wer lucky ter get yer job at Mac's back. Yew'll lose that at rate yer gowin . . .

STEVEN: Luck dint cum in ter it. A'm a good werker. (*Pause.*) Yew shunt be smokin'.

JULIE: If yew can drink, a can smoke. (*She takes a drag and stubs out the fag.*)

STEVEN: Woman. A'm doin all a can ter keep firm afloat. A've borrowed right left an' centre. A do ev'ry bit a ova'time cumin. The taxi-in. W'at abowt . . .

JULIE: W'at abowt the friggin taxi-in? Yer lost that job. It wer't job or yer licence. A'm not sure all this ova'time's ova'time. Yer a liar Steven. An' a never see yer.

STEVEN: So a 'ave a drink now an' again.

JULIE: Now an' again? Now an' again? Yer drinkin yer sen soft in't 'ead. A wunt care if a dint luv yer. It's because a luv yer a care.

STEVEN (*reaches for his drink*): If yer luved me yer'd leave me alone ter get on we these.

JULIE: Steven, yer not doin this fer me. (*Pause.*) Listen ter me w'en am talkin. A never asked yer. A wa 'appy. It's all in yer 'ead. (*Pause.*) Steven. Will yew listen. A need ter 'ave yer 'ere. We me. Sober. W'at d'yer think this is? Wind?

STEVEN: A know it's not wind. A've known fer months it's not wind.

JULIE: Yer allus sayin there's time. We need a bit more cash . . .

STEVEN: Luk luv. Yew've no idea . . .

JULIE: An' yer allus pissin up the wall . . .

STEVEN: A'm werkin me balls off . . .

JULIE: Well there is n'mor time. In three months a'm gunna 'ave this kid . . . .

STEVEN: We're bankrupt. (*Pause.*) It's cum at worst time.

JULIE: That's it in't it? You bloody resent it. Yew think a planned it. (*Pause. Shouts.*) Dunt yer? Dunt yer?

STEVEN: Luv. The neighbours.

JULIE (*shouts*): Sod the neighbours. (*Pause.*) W'at do yew care w'en yer cum in singin an' legless. (*Pause. Shouts.*) Yer resent it. Dunt yer?

STEVEN *springs to his feet. The things in his lap go flying. He's unsteady on his feet.*

STEVEN (*shouting*): Luk woman. A dunt resent it. A fuckin luv it. D'yer 'ear me? A luv the thing. (*Pause.*) A know it wern't fuckin planned. If it wer yew wunt be 'avin it now. Wud yer?

JULIE: That's it yer bastard. Yew think it's a mistake. A mistake. (JULIE *shouts at the neighbours.*) D'yer 'ear that ev'rywun? Our kid's a mistake. A mistake.

STEVEN: Julie.

JULIE (*shouts*): A bloody big . . .

STEVEN *slaps* JULIE. *She straightens up and slaps him. He draws back his hand to slap her again, stops, spins, and kicks his chair.*

STEVEN: If a ever get me 'ands on that bastard. A'll paste 'is shadow to the wall. A fuckin year's werk. A'll bury 'im.

JULIE: Oh yeah . . . Blame 'im. Blame 'im. (*She pats her stomach.*) A suppose yer blame 'im fer this. (*She shouts at the neighbours.*) Steven's a daddy an' 'e neva saw't stork cumin. Mummy din't tell 'im 'ow . . .

STEVEN (*as he shakes her he shouts*): Shut up. Shut up.

They topple. JULIE *lands badly.* STEVEN *is unhurt.* JULIE's *in pain.*

JULIE *lies on the floor.* STEVEN *tries to touch her.*

A'm sorry luv. A dint mean ter . . .

JULIE: Fuck off pig. Fuck off. (*Shouting causes her pain.*)

STEVEN: Are yer all reet luv?

STEVEN *stands over* JULIE.

JULIE: Dunt be a nob end. A dew this fer a laugh. (*Pause.*) Get me sum watta. Now Steven. (*Pause.*) Now.

STEVEN *runs to the kitchen.* JULIE *slides across the floor. She props her back against her chair. She shouts:*

Hurry up.

STEVEN: Drink it. Go on. Drink it luv.

JULIE *takes her pill container from her pocket.*

Yer not supposed ter . . .

JULIE: Fuck off. (*She washes down the pill.*) A suppose . . . yer blame . . . Tony fer this.

STEVEN *stoops to try and kiss* JULIE.

Dunt toch . . . me. A can dew . . . it . . . me sen.

She drags herself into her chair. STEVEN *stands over her and stares. He's wobbly on his feet.*

Big man. Big . . . bloody . . . man.

JULIE: Go on . . . oow d'yer blame . . . oow yer gunna kill?

STEVEN: It's n'wuns fault. It wer an accident.

JULIE: That's reet. Blame n'wun . . . There's n'wun tew blame . . . but yer sen.

STEVEN: Luk luv. A'm sorry.

JULIE: Sorry. Not as sorry as I am.

STEVEN: 'E were fiddlin from't off. A cun't understand it. We'd orders. We'd . . .

JULIE: W'at yew on abowt? (*Pause.*) Yer

sorry? Yer actin like yer just stood on me toe.

STEVEN: Everythin wer goin real. A'll we'd ter dew were . . .

JULIE (*shouts*): Yer still blamin . . . Ohoow oh. Fuckin 'ell . . . Blamin Tony. Yer dunt blame 'im. Yer envy 'im.

STEVEN: Yer talkin' rubbish. A dunt envy 'im.

JULIE: He got out . . . We're in't shit. Yer can't blame 'im fer't way yer treat me. Yer a drunk. (*Pause.*) Oh Steven. Yew werk 'ard . . . but yer . . . think we yer back.

STEVEN: A'm gunna find 'im.

JULIE: W'at yer dunna dew then? 'Ave a game a snooker we 'im?

STEVEN: A'll knock 'is fuckin 'ead off.

JULIE: Oh bloody 'ell. The big bloody man.

STEVEN: A'm not a big man. Dunt call me that. (*Pause.*) A'm a little man . . .

JULIE: Little man we big dreams . . .

STEVEN: A am sorry. 'Onestly luv. We can make things werk. A dunt 'ave ter drink. (*Pause.*) D'yer want mor watta?

JULIE: Oh Steven . . . Luk around yer. It used ter be . . . yew werked tew'ard . . . ter see me. W'at Tony wer doin . . . us . . . anythin. Now yer just . . . tew drunk.

STEVEN *is slumped in his chair, tears on his cheeks.* JULIE *wraps her arms around herself, holds tight against the pain.*

Lights fade to black.

Scene Eight

Saturday, early evening, November 1974.

STEVEN *is in the kitchen.* JULIE *is in her chair. The bulge has disappeared. At the back of the room, next to the*

certificate, is a vase of flowers. On the
floor, beside the cupboard, a suitcase.

STEVEN: Will ham sandwiches dew? Yer
can . . .

JULIE: A dunt mind . . .

STEVEN: A've w'at yer like . . .

JULIE: A'd like summat warm . . .

STEVEN: W'at abowt a cheese toasty. A
can warm that up. A 'am an' cheese
toasty? Yer like them. Why dunt yer
see w'at's on't telly? There might be a
film on.

JULIE: 'Ave yew got a paper?

STEVEN: It's on me chair. (*Pause.*) A-a
luv. We've got n'bread.

JULIE: Steven. This is Thursday's paper.

STEVEN: A've Sat'dey's in me coat
pocket.

STEVEN *rushes in from the kitchen.*
Yew sit back w'er yer wer. A'll ger'it.
A've opened it at telly page.

He puts his hand on her shoulder as he
gives her the paper. She takes the
paper. She pushes his hand from her
shoulder. This movement is deliberate
and final.
There's sum Ryvita. Will they do?

JULIE: Anythin Steven. A'll 'ave
anythin.

STEVEN: All reet luv. Ryvita. We 'am an'
cheese. A've sum toms. Yer can 'ave
them tew.

STEVEN *hesitates. He wants to touch*
JULIE. JULIE *reads the telly page*
with over-intense concentration.
Owt on? (*Pause.*) A've got a choc'late
cake. Yer like them luv.

JULIE: 'Ow did yer manage w'ile a wer
away?

STEVEN: Dunt yer want Ryvita? A cud
gow ter't chippy. Ten minutes.

JULIE: Is that w'at yer did? Ett chips
all't time?

STEVEN: A ett in't werks canteen. Yer
can ger' a three-course meal fer a
dollar. Berra then school dinnas.
(*Pause.*) Are yer all reet luv? D'yer like
yer flowers? (*Pause.*) A know yer like
flowers. (*Pause.*) A wer gunna bring
em tew yer t'neet. Good job a
phoned. First a 'eard. (*Pause.*) A
brought flowers all't time. Nurse sed
she'd enuff flowers fer ev'rywun.

JULIE: Aye.

STEVEN: D'yer like 'em?

JULIE: They're all reet.

STEVEN: A knew yer liked flowers.

JULIE: Steven. A'm 'ungry.

STEVEN: Yew'd lots a cards. (*Pause.*)
Well five. That's a lot ter say we din't
tell n'wun.

JULIE: Steven. A'm 'ungry. A luv cards.
A luv flowers.

STEVEN *goes to the kitchen.*
(*Rhythmically and bitterly.*) A luv
cards. A luv flowers. Only ever get 'em
w'en summat bad 'appens. Sight ov
'em meks me think 'am sick. (*She*
imitates STEVEN's *voice.*) Are yer
all reet luv? (*Pause.*) Cretin. A'm all
reet. A'm a bloody pools winner, me.

STEVEN: W'at yer say? (*Pause.*) W'at yer
say luv?

JULIE: A sed there's nowt on. There's
bloody nowt on.

STEVEN (*shouts*): Well neva mind luv.
He carries in the Ryvita with ham and
cheese and tomatoes. Beside it is a
chocolate cake. He puts them on the
coffee-table.
Neva mind. 'Ave sum Ryvita instead.

JULIE: Tea, Steven. A want sum tea.

STEVEN: A'll put kettle on.

JULIE: A'm thirsty now. A'll 'ave watta.

STEVEN: It's n'bother luv. A'll meck tea.

JULIE: Steven. A'm 'ungry now. A

wanna eat now. It's tew bloody dry. Just gee me watta. A'll 'ave tea later.

STEVEN *goes to the kitchen.*

JULIE (*shouts*): Steven. Why ampt yer gor'owt in?

STEVEN (*shouts*): A dint know. A dint know yer wer cumin owt.

JULIE (*shouts*): Yer sed yer phoned.

STEVEN (*shouts*): A did. Bur'a wer at werk.

JULIE (*shouts*)' Yer cudda got summat on't way.

STEVEN *starts back to the front room. He has two mugs of water.*

STEVEN (*shouts*): A wa . . .

JULIE: Place is a tip. Yer went ter't pub. Din't yer?

STEVEN: 'Ave this. Gow on.

JULIE: Yer went ter't pub.

STEVEN (*flops back into his chair*): A wa. (*Pause.*) A did yer . . . a wa afraid.

JULIE: Afraid a w'at?

STEVEN: A'wer afraid. Last month's bin't worst a me life.

JULIE: Well yew've nowt ter be afraid ov now. It's bloody dead in't it?

STEVEN: A know that. A'm not stupid. But since the accident.

JULIE: It wern't the fall Steven. It wern't the bloody fall. So yer can gee ova we yer 'A'm sorry luv. A'm sorry.'

STEVEN: But l am sorry.

JULIE: Yer not sorry. Yer bloody guilty.

STEVEN: A'm not guilty. (*Pause.*) Anyroads. Ow dew yew know it wunt fall? (*Pause.*) Stop playin we it. A thought yer wer 'ungry luv.

JULIE: A know. Because doctor told me. 'E sed if it wer't fall a'd ov 'ad baby there an' then. Not two bloody weeks later.

STEVEN: Can they tell things like that?

JULIE: A dunt know.

STEVEN: Shall a put yer case away?

JULIE: Leave it wer it is.

STEVEN: Shall a put a record on?

JULIE: Dunt be bloody stupid.

STEVEN: Luv. 'Ave sum cake instead.

JULIE (*bangs the arm of her chair*): Yer not bloody listenin. (STEVEN *sits.*) They sed it mite'a bin't pills. It mite'a bin't smokin . . .

STEVEN: A told yew yew wer . . .

JULIE: Yer told me nowt. D'yer 'ear me? Nowt.

STEVEN: Anywun knows smokin's n'gud.

Short silence.

JULIE: They sent me tew a psychiatrist.

STEVEN: W'at they dew that fer? Yer not mad.

JULIE: A know a'm not mad. Yew meck me mad. (*Pause.*) They sent me tew a woman called Mrs Hammond.

STEVEN: W'at did psychiatrist say?

JULIE: That wer Mrs Hammond. (*Pause.*) She told me a wa under stress. A bloody knew that already. That's w'at pills wer fer.

STEVEN: Did yer tell 'er that?

JULIE (*shouts*): Shut up. (*Pause.*) She sed it wer cuz a stress a lost the baby. An it wer cuz a stress a wer smokin s' much.

STEVEN: A thought pills wer fer ter cure it?

JULIE (*shouts*): Shut up. Bloody shut up. She sed a wa teckin tew many cuz a wa under stress.

Short silence.

STEVEN: Aye. Well. Go on. Now yew've got me shut up.

JULIE: She asked me if we wanted the kid.

STEVEN: W'at yer say? Yes?

JULIE: A told her a did. But yew dint.

STEVEN: Yer teld her w'at?

JULIE: A told her yew dint want it. She wants yew ter gow an' see 'er.

STEVEN: Yer are mad woman. W'at yer gow an' tell 'er that fer? Ow can a see 'er now? (*Pause.*) W'at yer tell 'er that for?

JULIE: A teld 'er ev'rythin. She sed it'd be a great 'elp. An' it wer.

STEVEN: A'm not gunna see n'loony doctor. There's nowt wrong we me.

JULIE: Yer a bloody idiot. That'll dew fer a start. She wants ter talk abowt our marriage.

STEVEN: Dunt call me an idiot woman. Ower marriage is nowt ter dew we'er. A'm doin me best.

JULIE: A teld 'er abowt yer drinkin. A teld 'er ow yer wunt cum near me cuz a wer pregnant.

A teld 'er abowt Elaine Carter.

STEVEN: Did yer tell 'er it wer bloody rubbish?

JULIE: A teld 'er abowt it. She sed it dint matter if it wer true or not. It 'ad a bearin on me state a' mind.

STEVEN: Yew w'at?

JULIE: A bearin on me state a'mind.

STEVEN: Now it's yew oow's an idiot. It's not bloody true. So ow can it matter? That bitch . . . A shud. She shud. She shud know better then tyin yer brain in knots.

JULIE: She wunt tryin ter tie me brain in knots. She wer tryin ter untie it. Yer gunna bloody see 'er.

STEVEN: A'm bloody not. Ow can a? Yer teld 'er ev'rythin. Yer neva asked me wunce. A wa there each neet. Yer cud'a sed summat. A'm gunna luk a reet prick.

JULIE: Steven. If yew dunt go a'm off. A'm off anyroads. (*Pause,*) A sed a'd try. She sed yer prob'ly wunt cum. She'll cum 'ere. A teld 'er ev'rythin. W'en yer 'it me. Abowt the red

nightie. A knew it wer a laugh. She sed yer'd problems we . . .

STEVEN (*shouts*): Yer teld 'er't lot. Did yer tell 'er't size a me dick? A ought ter give yer a thumpin. Yew've med me owt the twat. A ought ter gow an' smack that cow.

JULIE *pummels the arms of her chair with both fists. She kicks the chair's front with her heels.*

JULIE (*shouts*): Steven. Steven. (*Pause.*) Cun't yer just gow fer me. Fer us. Fer bloody me Steven.

STEVEN: A'm goin fer a drink.

JULIE: Fuckin typical.

STEVEN: Fuck off.

JULIE: Yer not goin . . . me case is packed . . . A'm gunna stay at me mum's . . .

JULIE *wraps herself around* STEVEN.

STEVEN: Ger off me . . .

JULIE: Yer gunna stay. Talk. Sort summat owt . . .

STEVEN: Fuck off . . .

JULIE: Nooh. Yer not goin. Yer . . .

STEVEN *smashes his palm against* JULIE's *face.* JULIE *loses her grip of* STEVEN *and slumps to the ground.* STEVEN *towers over her.*

STEVEN: Yer pushed me tew fuckin far . . .

JULIE *clutches her face.*

JULIE (*shouts*): Fuck off. Fuck off. Fuck off.

STEVEN *hunts out his coat.* JULIE *recovers.*

STEVEN (*shouts from the stair-bottom*): A'm goin ter't pub.

JULIE (*shouts*): Dunt cum back.

STEVEN *walks to the back of the front room.*

STEVEN: A'll be back fer me dinna.

JULIE: The fuckin place u'll be fuckin

locked. An' a wunt be fuckin 'ere.

STEVEN *turns to leave.* JULIE *flings an ashtray. It misses* STEVEN *and crashes into the wall at head height.* STEVEN *spins, slams his fist into the flower vase. It and the certificate crash to the floor. He slams the door.* JULIE *crawls to her certificate. She's crying.*

JULIE: Julie Tate. (*She can't get the words out easy. She's totally fucked.*) Shepton Secondary Modern. Advanced Swimming Certificate. Bastard. (*Pause. She puts the certificate on the cupboard. Shouts.*) Bastard. (*She pulls herself up and runs to the window. She flings it open. Shouts.*) A 'ate yer. A 'ate yer Steven. D'yer 'ear me? A fuckin 'ate yer. (*She slams the window.*) A wunt be 'ere . . . Not me . . . N'mor luv . . . Nooh. Luk at me little 'ouse. A luv me little 'ouse. A luv flowers. (*She bends and starts to pick the flowers up.*) A luv it. Me little 'ouse. (*She puts the vase on the cupboard. As she speaks, she puts the flowers in the vase one by one.*) A wunt be 'ere . . . Wun potata . . . Two potata . . . Three potata . . . Four. (*She clutches all but one of the flowers and crams them in the vase.*) Back fer me dinna? Four potatas make a bunch. An' so d'many mor. N'mor Steven. N'mor bloody bunches. (*She makes a fist and looks at it.*) Sort summat owt. Summat's gunna get sorted owt 'ere. Sorted out Steven. (*She picks up the last flower.*) We're gunna sort it owt. That Mrs Hammond. She sed. (*Pause.*) We're gunna sort it out. (*She puts the last flower in the vase.*) Five potatas. (*Pause.*) It'll 'ave a bearing this.

A low whispered chant begins. As the lights fade to black the chant's volume increases.

KIDS (*off*): Wun potata. Two potata. Three potata. Four. Four potatas make a bunch. An so dew many more.

(*Repeat.*)

If a quick change from Scene Eight to Scene Nine is possible then snap off the chant as the lights for Scene Nine snap on. If not, snap off the chant as the lights for Scene Eight snap to black.

JULIE (*as she walks into the kitchen*): Yer can't eat peas we a fork. (*Pause.*) It'll all 'ave a bearin. (*She slams the pin and board down on the table.*) Sort it owt Steven. Me state a mind. N'mor bunches. (*She unlids the container; tips some pills onto the board. She pushes them to the centre of the board.*) Wer gunna sort these potatas owt Steven. Sort 'em out.

She rolls the pills against the board; short jabs with the pin.

As this action establishes itself:

Slow light fade.

Snap to black.

Blackout.

Scene Nine

Monday, soon after Scene Three.

STEVEN *is in his chair. His head is slumped to the right. His mouth hangs open. On his chair is a plate of shepherd's pie and tomatoes. On the coffee-table is* JULIE's *empty plate. As she speaks,* JULIE *is kneeling beside* STEVEN. *She forks tiny clouds of mash in his open mouth.*

JULIE: Yew've let if g'cold.

They tumble from his mouth and down his chest.

N'wunder yer dunt want it.

She sticks the fork in the pie. She leaves it there like the handle of an inverted pan.

It's all't same ter me. A can allus warm it up.

She goes to the kitchen, throws the meal in the bin.

Oh. Fuckin 'ell.

She slides the dishes into the sink. She takes her pills from the kitchen table, looks at them and puts them down. She takes a drink of water by sticking her head under the tap. She splashes her face, dries herself on a dishcloth and goes into the front room.

Yew used ter blame't pills. Dint yer? Well it wern't all't pills. (*Pause.*) It wer yew an' yer bloody beer. (*Pause.*) Yer med me feel like a prize trollop. Me lay there all werked up. (*Softly.*) Time's a med me sen nice fer yew. (*Pause.*) A'd be thinkin. 'T'neet. It'll be different t'neet.' Sat there like a fruit cake. Fer 'ours. (*Pause.*) A'd get s'bloody angry a'd just get back in me 'ousecoat. (*Pause.*) Worse'd de me all ova yew. Yer med me feel like . . . like wun'a them mymph-a-metics. (*Pause.*) 'A'm sorry luv.' That'd be yew. Slurrin' owt at corner of yer mouth. (*Imitates a drunken slur.*) Sowwey-luv-am-nor-up-tew-it. Pilla'd reak like a fuckin brewery. Quite the man yew wer. A right Clint Eastwood. Man enuff ter go chasin that Elaine-cow-faced-Carter.

The neighbour knocks. JULIE shouts, but not in reply to the neighbour. It's a continuation of her tirade.

'Nutin 'appened. A bit a fun luv.'

Loud knocking from the neighbour. JULIE turns sharply. Pause.

Tsk. (*Quietly.*) Know w'at Steven? A bloody believe yer. Why not? It wer't story a my life. Me bloody sex-life anyroads. Nuthin bloody 'appened. Yer'd cheek ter dress me like a bloody tramp. (*Pause.*) N'bdey forced me. It wer a giggle. A suppose it wer fer yew. Yer Pink Lady in a bright red dress. (*Pause.*) Then yer'd gee me, 'It's not reet luv. It dunt feel reet we yew.' Well oow did it feel reet we Steven? (*Pause.*) If yer'd a only touched me. Brought me summat. Flowers. Choc'lates. Even a bloody record. (*Pause.*) If yew'd a

sed ter me wunce, 'Yew luk nice', yer'd a made my day. (*Long pause.*) A'm bloody gasping.

She runs to the kitchen. She searches through the bin. She finds a longish dogend. She smokes it down in a few sharp drags. She stands at the front-room door.

D'yer want a drink? A do. 'An a'm gunna 'ave wun. Yew know them classical music records? (*Pause.*) Them wuns ye mum got yer fer Christmas. Yer neva play 'em. A knew yew wunt luk there. (*She pulls out -- triumphantly -- a quarter bottle of vodka and two thin wine glasses.*) Oh aye. That wer't best. Yer shuda 'eard yer mum. (*She sloshes out two large vodkas. Imitates a northern woman faking a BBC accent.*) 'Little mahn chan't help it.' (*She puts STEVEN's glass on the coffee-table.*) 'Hour Steven 'as hallus longer'ed fer sumthin a little better'n all this.' 'Really,' a sez. 'Ard faced cow. A allus wanted a yacht. But this. Bloody this. This is my little 'ouse. (*Louder.*) Her stood there. On that bloody rug. (*As she thrusts out her hand to point out the rug she spills vodka from her glass.*) Oh bloody 'ell. (*She glares at the mess.*) In my 'ome. (*Mimicking.*) 'Yes well daharling. Yew know how men are.' A'd ter bite me lip. It wer all a cud dew not ter say, 'A know 'ow yer little boy is.' 'And daharling,' she sez, 'daharling. There's no need tew swear.' W'er does she? The tart of a poxy scrap-metal merchant. Jumble-sale Lil. The rag 'n' bone man's fancy bit. Where's she get 'daharling' from? (*She shouts.*) The fuckin' wet 'ead.

The neighbour knocks.

(*Screaming.*) All reet. All reet. A bloody 'ear yer. Dunt get yer knickers in a twist.

The neighbour knocks.

(*Screaming.*) Betta still. Keep 'em on. A wud if a wer yew.

She stomps into the kitchen. She rummages through the bin for a dogend. She can't find one. She eats a pill and swills it down with vodka. She goes out to her position by the front-room window. She looks from the edge of drawn curtains. She looks at STEVEN.

A can't tell. If it's dark outside. Or if it's gone dark. In me. (*Pause.*) A'm sorry luv. A'm sorry.

She rests her hand on the back of STEVEN'*s chair. She stoops to kiss his neck and cheek. Her lips are uncertain and awkward. She tries to squeeze into the chair beside* STEVEN. *He takes up too much space. She bends to the arm of the chair and tries to brush her breast against his hand. She lifts his hand to her breast. She lets go of his hand and his dead arm flops down. She holds herself over him. Her palms pressed into the arms of the chair. Her legs astride him. Drunkenness steals her balance. She recovers. She takes a glass from the coffee-table. She sits on the arm of* STEVEN'*s chair and strokes his neck and hair.*

'Ave a drink Steven. Fer me. Please. Just a little bit.

She puts the glass down on the floor by STEVEN'*s chair. She resumes stroking.*

A allus wanted kids. An' fer us ter be 'appy. We wunt goin anyw'ere. But it's different fer kids. Now anyway. They gow ter school. Not like we did. They tek it serious. Tint just a bit a paper they gee yer at fourteen. (*Long pause.*) If we neva got anyw'er. If Jubilee Bikes wer allus . . . Jubilee Bikes. If we'd kids. At least we'd a been part a summat that wer goin sumw'ere. (*Pause.*) There's n'point in werkin inter't ground fer summat that wunt cumin. We wer miserable. We'd a bin buggered be't time we got there. (*Pause.*) But we kids. We'd a bin part a summat. A future.

She looks up at the roof. She stands. She takes off her house coat. Beneath it is the red nightie. She bunches up the housecoat to form a pillow. She puts it at the end of the hearth-rug. As she moves she speaks.

Yew'd say. Not yet. Can't afford it. Gotta get the bis'ness goin. Get it toddling. W'at yer wer sayin wer, we can't afford a future. (*Pause.*) A'm a bit flushed up. (*Pause.*) A ampt 'ad time ter change. Not since other day. (*She pulls* STEVEN *from his chair. His weight is difficult for her to manage. She knocks over the vodka glass.*) Bugger it. A'll ger it tomorra.

She hauls him down and lays his head on the pillow. She recovers her breath and walks around the house locking all the windows and doors. Slow light fade as she does this. She mumbles about the neighbour. Eventually she lays down beside STEVEN.

Total darkness.

Scene Ten

Tuesday, 10.00 a.m., the next day.

JULIE *is at the front-room window. She sips at a cup of tea. There's a mug beside* STEVEN. *His corpse is in his chair, a copy of the Mirror in his lap.* JULIE *hasn't slept. Her hair is uncombed. She is hungover. She knocks on the window. Pauses. Knocks again. Unlocks and opens the window.*

JULIE: Tommy? 'Ave . . .

TOMMY (*off*): Hiya luv. Nice ter see yer owt. Are yer all reet? Ower Sheila wer gunna cum 'an see yer. But we't kids an' that . . .

JULIE: Yerh. A'm. A'm all reet. But . . .

TOMMY (*off*): If it's abowt ower Jimmy. 'Ave told the little bugger. 'E'll get n'sympathy frum me. 'E's far tew cheeky. Gee 'im a clip. If yer can't catch 'im, cum an' tell me. A'll turn 'is arse red.

JULIE: No. It's er. . .

TOMMY (*off*): If it's abowt yer Steven. Ower Jimmy sed 'e wunt well. A wa gunna cum round an' see 'im.

JULIE: Nooh. (*Pause.*) 'Ave yer got any fags? A dunt want ter . . .

TOMMY (*off*): Sorry luv. Dunt mind me manners. A wa on't pop last neet. Ower Sheila's bin up an' down we't vac. It's only way ter get me up.

JULIE: It's all reet. Yer can jus' pass 'em threw't window.

TOMMY (*off*): Nay luv. Tint n'bother. A'll be round side in a tic.

JULIE *closed and locks the window.*

TOMMY (*off, by the side door*): A up Julie. It's me, luv.

JULIE *stays where she is.*

TOMMY (*knocks*): Julie? Julie?

JULIE *crosses the room She closes the door behind her. She does not look back. She has her tea-cup in her hand.*

TOMMY (*off*): Julie? Fag man's 'ere.

JULIE *unlocks the door and lets TOMMY in.*

JULIE: There's nowt wrong we'im yer know. 'E's asleep.

TOMMY: Aye luv. There's fags. They'll dew fer yer fer now?

JULIE: Yew've still got yer tan.

TOMMY: Ohwer. Year. But yer shuda seen us w'en we first got back. Me an' ower Sheila wer like a couple a Pakies. We'd a real time. (*Pause.*) 'Ere. Is that a fresh pot? Me mouth's as dry as a leper's bandage.

JULIE: A med it a few minutes ago. Cum in't kitchen.

He enters

TOMMY: Crackin. As long as it's wet an' warm.

TOMMY *investigates the tea-pot.* JULIE *takes a fag from the packet. She lights it on the third match.*

A saw Steven. Up club. Sat'dey. 'E wer steemin be time a got there. A wa all over yesterdey. A din't see 'im n'w'ere. A wa supposed ter be in werk this . . .

JULIE: Tommy.

Short silence.

TOMMY: 'Im an' Sam. They wer puttin't little 'uns away. They can both teck it . . .

Short silence.

JULIE: We're on 'is own?

TOMMY: No luv. 'E wer we Sam. Sam Shaw.

JULIE: 'E dint gow owt last neet.

TOMMY: That'll be it then. 'E'll be sober. N'wonder 'e's . . .

JULIE: A luv 'im Tommy.

TOMMY: A thought 'e'd be . . . Aye. A know yer dew.

JULIE: A luv 'im. D'yer understand?

TOMMY: Aye, 'course. A well luv. A've ter gow now. A'll be . . .

JULIE: D'yer want ter see 'im?

TOMMY: A wunt wake 'im.

JULIE: 'E's in't front room. Yer can teck a peek.

TOMMY: A'll just say 'ello. If 'e's awake like.

TOMMY *opens the door to the front room and stares in.*

TOMMY (*quietly*): All reet lad? Julie sez yer a bit under. (*To* JULIE.) It smells luv.

JULIE *hands* TOMMY *a cigarette.*

Why've yer all't windas closed? Open wun up luv. (TOMMY *walks to the centre of the front room. He talks as he lights his fag.*) Go on luv. Let sum air in.

JULIE *begins to cry, very very simple tears.*

JULIE: Things ampt bin. (*Pause.*) A din't want nun ov 'is (*Pause.*) moods.

(*Pause.*) Ther' wer summat ter say.

JULIE *is beside the window.* TOMMY *crouches beside* STEVEN.

TOMMY: A'yer reet lad?

TOMMY *reaches to touch* STEVEN. *But he hesitates.*

JULIE: A wunt leavin 'im fer eva. A needed a rest. (*Pause.*) A thought 'e'd just sleep.

TOMMY: Steven?

JULIE: Tint it yer know. 'E's just asleep. (*Pause.*) A kinda sleep.

TOMMY: 'Ave yer called a doctor?

JULIE: A dunt know w'at 'ad dew. A luv 'im. (*Pause.*) A . . . A . . . .

Silence.

TOMMY: 'E's bloody cold luv. (*Pause.*) A'm gunna call a doctor.

JULIE: A dint mean fer nun a this.

TOMMY: Get a blanket luv. Pur'it ova 'im.

JULIE: No. (*Pause.*) E dunt need a . . .

TOMMY: A'll send ower Sheila round. A'm gerrin a doctor.

JULIE: A dunt want n'wun round.

TOMMY *crosses to the door.* JULIE *is at his heel*

A dunt need. We dunt need. N'wun. D'yer understand Tommy? D'yer bloody understand?

TOMMY: Yeah luv. Yeah. A understand. Yew wait 'ere. We 'im.

TOMMY *exits at speed.* JULIE *follows to the door. As* TOMMY *leaves* JULIE *slams the door. She slumps against it.*

Fade to dark

JULIE (*quietly*): No.

Scene Eleven

Tuesday, soon after.

Sound is of immense value in this piece. Careful positioning of the speakers should be considered. We should 'hear'

this through JULIE'*s ears.*

One suggestion: Use a piece of jagged and distorted music, e.g. introduction to 'Pornography' by the Cure (Album: 'Pornography').

Second suggestion: Children's chants, distorted/electronically treated; 'Coming. Ready or not. Coming Ready or not.' Overdub: 'One potata. Two potata. Three potata. Four. Four potatas make a bunch. An' so do many more.'

Third suggestion: Cover the transition with a count. 'Five. Ten. Fifteen' etc.

All effort should be made to create an atmosphere of intimidation and collapse through the sound landscape.

Dark stage.

A single, dim, parallel spot, on JULIE.

JULIE *sits on the stairs. She is sobbing. She has a handbrush in one hand. Beside her is a bottle of bleach.*

Offstage murmur: a police radio. Crackle/static. Unclear message. Use call signs. Alpha Oscar Tango/Radio talk: Over and Out. Over.

JULIE: Fuck off. All ov yer. (*Pause.*) Non of yer knew 'im. (*Pause. Shouts.*) Piss of an' get stuffed.

Short silence.

From the area of the front window.

MALE COPPER (*off*): It's all reet luv. N'bdey's gunna 'urt yer.

Knocking at the front window.

Just let us in luv. You. Get round the back. (*Pause.*) Bring me the neighbour. The one who found them.

The crunch of metal on gravel. The sound of feet.

Check all the upstairs windows.

Lights fade in.

STEVEN *is in his chair. A blanket covers all of him except his neck and head.*

Open up luv. It's easiest in't end.

The sound of both doors being kicked.

JULIE *picks up the bleach and the brush. She runs out of the stair-door and snibs it. She backs away from the front window as though someone is there.*

Open up. Open up, Julie. This is the police. Open up.

The sound of glass breaking in the kitchen area.

JULIE *runs to the other front-room door; snibs it.*

JULIE: Yer not teckin 'im from me.

JULIE *swings to face the front window.*

The sound of breaking glass at the front-room window.

Bugger off. (*Pause. Shouts.*) Get out. Get out a my 'ouse.

JULIE *hurls the bleach at the front window.*

The sound of breaking glass. Both outer doors are being forced.

TOMMY (*off*): Julie. Julie. It's me. Tommy.

JULIE *runs to her chair and tries to pull it to block the door connecting the front room and hall. TOMMY flings himself against the front door. It caves in. He recovers and starts to kick in the stair-door.*

It's me. Tommy. It's Tommy

JULIE (*tries to pick up* STEVEN): Cum on Steven. Cum on. Fer me. Cum on.

TOMMY *caves in the stair-door.* JULIE *backs away to her corner.*

TOMMY: Careful Julie lass. Careful luv.

For a moment the two gaze at each other. JULIE *straightens up. A fragment of joy enters her. She pulls her brush back like a club. She starts to run forward.*

All noise stops on the instant of the blackout, all noise, that is, except JULIE's *scream. This begins at the instant of her running forward.*

A strobe flashes. (If possible freeze the movement in a series of jagged stills.)

She leaps on the coffee-table. The brush is a club in her hand.

Scream on all cylinders.

JULIE: Reeeeeeeeeeeeeeellllllleeeeeeeeeee-vvvooooooooooooooooooooooo.

Strobe out.

Total blackness.

Give a few seconds for the final image to settle. Play the opening bars of Presley's ballad 'All That I Am'.

Cut the song.

As the theatre empties play the rest of the song.

SMITH

by Johnnie Quarrell

For Kathy

Characters

SMITH, *a black prisoner*
DOCTOR
FAIRBRASS, *senior prison officer*
ROBERTSON, *junior prison officer*

Production note:
The play requires no set.
Special attention to lighting, and the
very minimum of props.

ACT ONE

Scene One

A prison yard. The sound of a Black Maria reversing. Late evening. PRISON OFFICER ROBERTSON *enters. He gives direction to driver of vehicle, off.*

ROBERTSON: Easy! A couple of yards . . . That'll do you nicely! (*He goes off and unlocks the Maria to let the prisoner out. Off.*) Step down and stand over there! Be quick! Haven't got all bloody night . . .

SMITH, *a black prisoner, enters, visibly shaken.* ROBERTSON *follows after* SMITH.

Right. You just stand over there while I see the Maria out . . . (*He calls off.*) Take it away! Right hand down! That's it!

The sound of the vehicle leaving. ROBERTSON *circles* SMITH.

Well, then, who have we here . . ? No ordinary specimen I see . . . The guard and the driver said you caused quite a skirmish when they tried to put you into the Black Maria . . . That probably accounts for the blood on your fancy shirt . . . Mind you, if you're not one for tight places, it is a bit cramped in the old black box . . . The rest of your clothes are extravagant as well aren't they? Are you some sort of an actor?

SMITH *nods 'no'.*

Oh. Well you're a very loud dresser all the same.

SMITH *nods 'yes'.*

Your name's Smith, is that correct?

SMITH: Mr ordinary Smith . . . With one S, one M, one I, one T, and one H.

ROBERTSON (*false laugh*): Ha ha ha. Now I know why you are in those fancy clothes: a clown. I bet you've got a funny nose in your pocket. Clowns never really made me laugh, actually . . . all the same, Smith's a

funny name for a black man. (*Pause.*) What might you do for a living then? You haven't come here because you're a thief. What you did is very odd. (*Pause.*) So what do you do for a living? I'm very interested . . . Mr Smith. (*Pause.*) I'm listening.

SMITH: Although I'm ordinary in name and rank . . . I can be extraordinary in thought and feeling. I can act many parts.

ROBERTSON: Yes, but that doesn't tell us very much about you, does it? I'm going to be watching you for the next few weeks and I like to know about the men under my . . . custodial care. Unlike some I know . . . so tell me more.

SMITH (*pause*): Of my ordinary, or extraordinary life?

ROBERTSON: A bit of both, eh? I'll figure it out afterwards . . .

SMITH (*pause*): My ordinary life . . . and world . . . consists of a . . . fish bowl. You know the ones I mean?

ROBERTSON: Oh, yes . . . Well just listen to me. I wanted this to be a serious . . . little chat. I want to know something about you. If you don't want a little bit of mutual understanding to pass between us, that's up to you.

SMITH: I'm telling you about my ordinary life.

ROBERTSON: Yeah, and you're a little goldfish swimming around in circles . . . getting nowhere. Right? Join the club, mate!

SMITH: Not exactly.

ROBERTSON: What then?

SMITH: I'm a medium-sized black man swimming around in a white man's world . . . looking for food and shelter. Seeking the Lord. (*Pause.*) I lived in Hackney once . . . I lived in Kingston, Jamaica, once. Once is very long ago. Once is no fixed abode. Once I lived in cool luxury . . . I was surrounded by good things . . . Clothes in all the wardrobes . . . On the dummies. On the women. (*Pause. He smiles.*) Off the women. I lived in a bright world of fabrics and . . . jazz. Promenades that shot out in all directions . . . Girls and boys with grace shaking their arses at the . . . dimly lit faces of a thousand strangers. A none world, man. Of luxury and poverty. I hung back, an observer to my own . . . adversity . . .

ROBERTSON: Are you a male model?

SMITH: I'm a creator of body covering, man. I designed clothes.

ROBERTSON: Well all I can say is that your *behaviour* don't add up to the kind of man you say you are.

SMITH (*pause*): Ah. That's part of my extraordinary life.

ROBERTSON: Is it now?

SMITH: My ordinary life toppled me.

ROBERTSON: What happened?

SMITH (*pause*): I woke up one morning and asked a question.

ROBERTSON: What? What question?

SMITH: I got out of bed first. I was alone in the bed. Part of the condition . . . Then I went to the bathroom. (*Pause.*)

ROBERTSON: And?

SMITH (*pause*): I looked at myself in the mirror. And then I asked myself the question.

ROBERTSON: And the question was . . . ?

SMITH: The question was . . . to myself . . .

ROBERTSON: What was the sodding question for Christ sake!

SMITH: I said to myself: what is your life all about?

ROBERTSON: Was that all?

SMITH: It was enough.

ROBERTSON: What, to send you . . . To make you do what you did?

SMITH: It was a long time ago . . .

ROBERTSON: Not it wasn't, mate! It was yesterday. You done what you done yesterday. Then you got arrested, the Old Bill nicked you and you was in front of the magistrate this afternoon. He remanded you for a medical report.

SMITH (*pause*): It was a long time ago . . .

ROBERTSON: Yesterday I said!

SMITH: It was a long time ago when I asked the question. The mirror has cracked since then . . . The rent hasn't been paid. My mother died . . . I had no money to fly home . . . My life has lost its meaning. I only see the end of the story. Which is not the beginning . . . . But no one can touch my ordinary life . . . lying back as it does behind my extraordinary ways . . . But it has never removed my fear of the dark . . . I thought it would have done. I'm praying hard for the final solution.

ROBERTSON: If things are so grim, how come you can still dress like that? That's not ordinary gear.

SMITH: I got it on social security . . . I starved myself for six weeks to dress myself. You can't have it both ways . . .

ROBERTSON: Here, you're having me on, aren't you? You're not a black vicar in disguise are you? That would account for your behaviour. (*Pause.*) Are you? Come on, the truth this time.

SMITH nods 'no'.

Well what you did sounds very much like what a crazy vicar might do. Not the violent bit, but the other bit. All sorts of odd-balls in here, mate. You're just one of many. (*Pause.*) You haven't got much to say for yourself that might help matters, have you?

SMITH looks; nods 'no'.

Nerves I expect. Especially if it's the first time in prison. Affects some blokes very badly. It's the atmosphere you see. You bang the door on them, they nearly jump out of their skin. Remand's always a bit of a pig anyway.

Banged up in your cell twenty-three hours a day. Bad news for some . . . Mind you I can imagine what it must feel like . . . A bit suffocating . . .

SMITH: Jesus Christ . . .

ROBERTSON: What was that? What did you say?

SMTIH: I'm tired.

ROBERTSON: Well you're in for a three-week lay-down so you won't be able to use that one anymore.

SMITH: Can I get to a bed, man?

ROBERTSON: Don't come all that *man* stuff with me. I'm Mr Robertson to you. And you're Smith to me . . . That's a funny bloody name for a black person.

SMITH: You think so?

ROBERTSON: Don't you?

SMITH: For fuck sake! I'm tired!

ROBERTSON: Watch it, mate! I'm just saying that Smith's a funny name for a black person. All right!

SMITH: Oh, yeah . . . You're saying it nicely. Over and over . . .

ROBERTSON: That's right. That's it. (*Pause.*) And just to make sure we've got the right body, just answer yes or no to my questions. First, your name is Smith and you've been remanded for three weeks for a medical report. Correct?

SMITH: If that's what you say, that's what you say . . .

ROBERTSON: I said, correct?

SMITH (*pause*): Yeah . . .

ROBERTSON: They told the guard and the driver when they picked you up from the magistrates' court that you were violent. That you'd head-butted a copper. Is that right?

SMITH: Self-defence.

ROBERTSON: Arrogant bugger aren't you? They also said that you were doing press-ups in the middle of a busy main road with a bible on your back. Well?

SMITH: Yeah . . . (*He moves around.*)

ROBERTSON: Keep still. This is not an exercise yard.

SMITH (*stops*): Still.

ROBERTSON: And you do dress a bit . . . over the top don't you? A bit . . . gay, like. Are you a poof? That's it, isn't it?

SMITH (*pause*): I was raped when I was ten years old. I don't know what the fuck I am. Only the Lord knows.

ROBERTSON (*pause*): Bloody state of you . . . You better be careful . . . The other cons don't take kindly to poofters at the moment. Aids. A very tight community is a prison. I'm just warning you for your own good. Be warned.

SMITH: Listen, man. You hard up for a friend? OK. I'm your friend. Now can I go to my bed? I feel sick. I want to see a doctor.

ROBERTSON: Sick you say? What way, sick?

SMITH: Just sick! My mind is in . . . hell . . . I'm bad . . . (*He starts moving.*) I need forgiveness.

ROBERTSON: Keep bloody still when I'm talking to you!

SMITH (*gestures*): Still.

ROBERTSON: That's better. You'll have a medical check soon. After a shower, a general clean-up. You'll get some prison clothes. You can't go parading around a nick dressed like that. It'd cause a lot of trouble. (*Pause.*) You are a poof, aren't you?

SMITH (*pause*): What d'you think, man?

ROBERTSON: I think you're a poof. Not that it matters to me.

SMITH: Takes one to recognise one . . . I've heard it said . . .

ROBERTSON: Cheeky bastard, aren't you? I'm a married man!

SMITH: Anything you say. (*He starts moving.*)

ROBERTSON: Keep still I said! I've told you already! Got to learn to do what you're told. A bit of discipline. (*Pause.*) Right. I'll check the roll-call. Answer when I call your name. Smith?

SMITH: Yeah.

ROBERTSON: John William Smith?

SMITH: Right.

ROBERTSON: John William? That's coming it a bit.

SMITH: Arse-holes. I didn't name myself. . .

ROBERTSON: That's naughty! Very naughty. If our Mr Fairbrass hears that sort of language, you'll be more than sick, son. (*He circles* SMITH.) You don't know how lucky you are. Because you're a bit of a psycho, you'll be in a pad of your own on the sick wing. A lot of the cons are banged up three to a cell. You wouldn't like that. You can't fall over without touching the walls. There's twelve hundred men in here. It was built for eight hundred. How about that eh?

SMITH (*starts moving*): Maybe I should stay here . . .

ROBERTSON: Keep bloody still! How many more times must I tell you?

SMITH: Fuck you! I've been jammed in that Black Maria like this. (*He sits on the floor, grasps his legs under his chin.*) For over two hours! They don't even shift animals around in that sort of space! My body's dead! I've got to move . . .

ROBERTSON: Get up off your arse and keep still! Up!

SMITH (*stands*): He is risen . . .

ROBERTSON: You haven't been here five minutes and you're complaining already. Now you listen to me very carefully. When you come through these gates, you lose all the rights of a free man. Complaining is one of those rights. There is no one to listen to complaints in here. You take what's dished out to you, how it's dished out to you, when it's dished out to you and why it's dished out to you. Understood? I don't want to repeat myself. Just take it from me, that the less you say, the better it'll be. That's assuming you want a clear passage. Got me? Right. First we're going through reception. Then I'll take you across to the sick wing. In other words, you'll have a shower, see the doctor and then get banged up for the night. You understand?

SMITH (*nods*): I understand English, yes . . .

ROBERTSON: Right. Let's go then. That way, John William bloody Smith!

Both march off briskly.

Lights down quickly.

Scene Two

Empty stage. The sound of water – showers. ROBERTSON *stands rigid.*

ROBERTSON (*to* SMITH, *off*): You've got two minutes! (*Pause.*) Are you undressed? (*He looks.*) You're not even undressed! Look lively! I want to get home this evening. I'm not serving a bloody sentence . . . (*Pause.*) You've got one minute. After that, the water's off. (*Pause.*) Mr Fairbrass won't like it either . . . He'll be waiting for us over in the wing . . . He's bound to find something to moan about . . . A bit of a moaner is Mr Fairbrass . . . Any excuse, mate, and he's calling on Mr Wood. Then you are in trouble. (*He looks in the shower room.*) Did you hear me? (*Pause.*) I'm supposed to be going to the pictures tonight . . . last thirty seconds, Smith! (*Pause.*) That's it! If you're not clean now you never will be. (*He turns the water off.*) Water off! Let's have you!

SMITH (*enters, wet*): Cleanliness is next to godliness . . .

ROBERTSON: You're a religious nut, aren't you? Look, just dry your body and keep the towel wrapped around you.

SMITH (*looks*): Where are my clothes?

ROBERTSON: Your clothes are in a cardboard box. You won't see them again until you leave. You'll be fitted out with prison clothes. But first you've got the see the doctor. If you are religious, just pray that the old boy's not been hitting the whisky bottle. By Christ, he's one man who's as changeable as the weather. Working with you lot has done his head in, I think. Right, let's go then. Follow me!

Lights down.

Scene Three

Medical inspection: PRISON DOCTOR, ROBERTSON, SMITH. *The* DOCTOR *stands.*

ROBERTSON (*pushing* SMITH): Over there! Drop your towel and stand in front of the doctor. Stand up straight! The doctor wants to look at you.

He stands back. SMITH *stands naked. Pause.*

DOCTOR (*looks, takes a small torch from his pocket*): Name?

SMITH: Smith.

Pause.

DOCTOR: Smith. (*He stands behind* SMITH.) Bend over.

Pause. SMITH *looks at the torch.*

I said bend over.

ROBERTSON: Do what the doctor says, Smith!

The DOCTOR *looks at* ROBERTSON. SMITH *slowly bends over. The* DOCTOR *shines the torch on* SMITH's *behind.*

Stand straight again. (*He goes and faces* SMITH.) Arms up. (*He shines torch under his arms.*) Down.

SMITH *looks at* ROBERTSON. *The* DOCTOR *shines the torch on* SMITH's *private parts.*

Well then?

SMITH: Why are you shining that torch at me?

DOCTOR: Lice. I'm looking for lice. What's the matter with you?

SMITH: I'm sick.

DOCTOR: I know. That's why you're here. (*He rubs his hand over* SMITH.) Perspiration. Officer, this man is perspiring. He feels quite hot. It's a cold evening.

ROBERTSON: Just stepped from the shower, doctor.

DOCTOR: Oh. That explains it. I thought you might be taking drugs, Smith. That you might be . . . withdrawing . . . Do you use drugs? (*He looks at his arm quickly.*) I take a special interest in drug users. Your arms show no signs . . . On the scales.

SMITH *moves to the scales and stands rigid. The* DOCTOR *weighs him.*

Any serious loss of weight whilst you're in prison will be a fair indication as to your general health. Understood?

SMITH: Yeah.

DOCTOR (*pause*): Good. That'll do. Have you got anything to say to me?

SMITH (*looks at his own nudity*): I'm sick . . .

DOCTOR: Have you got anything to say to me that I don't already know!

SMITH *nods, confused.*

ROBERTSON: He's nodding, doctor.

DOCTOR (*pause*): Good. Take him to the sick-wing officer. I'll see him tomorrow.

SMITH: I don't like the darkness!

ROBERTSON: Be quiet, Smith! Pick up your towel and let's go! Move it.

SMITH (*to the* DOCTOR): I don't like the darkness . . .

He picks up his towel, covers himself. He walks off followed by ROBERTSON.

The DOCTOR *watches them leave. He is very agitated and throws his white coat off.*

Lights down.

Scene Four

The clothing store. A bundle of clothes on the floor. SMITH *is putting on a brown-style army suit. He sits on the floor to put on the boots.*

ROBERTSON: Just look at that, eh? Soles of your feet are white. How do you account for that?

SMITH: Arseholes . . . (*He continues to dress.*)

ROBERTSON: Hey! That's twice you've sworn at me! I'm not warning you again. Any more swearing and you'll be in serious trouble. Too big a chip on your shoulder, mate. There's me bending over backwards to be nice to you and see what thanks I get. One minute you're sick, the next minute, you're all aggressive. They told me the criminal mind was devious. It's certainly thankless. Well you just shove those boots on and stand up! You're making me hoarse having to keep shouting at you. Fairbrass doesn't waste his breath, I'll tell you that. Not him, mate. If Fairbrass *and* Mr Wood go to town on you . . . By Christ, you'll have a good reason to visit the doctor then. I've seen the senior officer cure the devious mind all right. You show him respect — or else. (*Pause.*) Have you understood what I've said? I can't spell it out any

clearer. It's more than my job's worth. Just hurry up. And remember what I've said! It's part of your survival kit.

SMITH (*points at his head*): It's been recorded, man.

ROBERTSON: And don't call me 'man'. I'm Mr Robertson.

SMITH: Here's to you . . . Mr Robertson . . . (*Long pause. He laces his boots.*) Rock of ages . . . Rock of fucking ages . . .

ROBERTSON: You're doing it again! You don't hear too good, do you? I said cut out the swearing! So cut it out!

SMITH: Not at you, mister . . . It's the rock . . . I'm swearing at the rock . . . I stood solid on the rock. God held me firm, placed me high on the rock, away from the crashing seas below. I stood majestic. Proud. Secure. Then a fierce wind came . . . out of time . . . through time . . . I had nothing to hold on to when life swept me away. The rock was solid. I knew that. I knew so I believed. Faith held me to the rock. But then came that fierce wind from the future . . . Lifted me up and tossed me about like . . . some old crumpled sweet wrapper. I came off the rock. And I hit the world. (*He stands.*) It was like I suddenly found myself naked and forgotten. Have you ever felt naked and forgotten? Off of the rock? In a world of . . . shit! Do you know what's it's like being naked in a pile of shit! Like a messy little child . . . without a mummy . . . without the cleansing hands . . . Oh, rock of ages . . .

ROBERTSON: We got all sorts in here, you know. There's nothing clever about you. Child molesters, incestuous fathers, religious nuts, petty nothings, alcoholics, junkies, the dregs of society. Sometimes we hold on to the hard nuts, just until they go to the big nicks. But this place . . . this is one of the dustbins of the penal system. Anybody who's a nobody who breaks the law comes here first, either to do a little bit, or wait a little bit.

SMITH: But before they're here — they're out there.

ROBERTSON: That's very true. The same men here as out there.

SMITH: If they're there before they're here . . . Is *there* like here?

ROBERTSON: This is a nick, mate!

SMITH (*pause*): And what's out there?

ROBERTSON: Ha! What you ain't got at the moment: freedom.

SMITH (*pause*): Ah . . . freedom. Yes. Tell me, mister, what if you have to beg, borrow or steal for your freedom. What then?

ROBERTSON: You get nicked. That's what!

SMITH (*pause*): Justice, eh?

ROBERTSON: I wouldn't know about that. Don't start getting heavy with me. I ain't in the mood. You're all the same, you blokes. You get nicked and then start talking about justice. Should have thought about justice before you broke the law.

SMITH: I haven't been found guilty, mister. I thought the law said I was innocent until proved otherwise.

ROBERTSON: A man with no fixed abode has to come here. Otherwise they'll never find you. Pity you wasn't a man of money. Could have got yourself a brief and he'd have got you bail. Then you wouldn't be here and I wouldn't be having to bloody well work late again. It's time we made a move. D'you realise I've been working since six this morning? Five hours over my official time. No wonder I get irritable and feel like I want to bash someone's brains out. Come on. I'll take you to the wing. Then I'll go and have my supper before I go to the pictures. Move it!

SMITH: Before we go, mister. I must tell you something.

ROBERTSON: Be quick!

SMITH: In here, in my heart, I know I'm not a guilty man. I know that.

ROBERTSON: Oh, for Christ sake! What does it matter what you know? It's not what you know. It's what *they* know.

SMITH: My conscience is clear. God knows that.

ROBERTSON: That won't stop them banging the door on you. I don't know what sort of a conscience you have got but you, apart from causing a traffic hold-up, head-butted a policeman. You're violent. Probably a very nasty piece of work altogether. Move!

SMITH: When I sit in the sun I burn.

ROBERTSON: You burn? Don't make me laugh! Come on!

They move off.

Lights down.

Scene Five

The prison wing. SMITH *stands centre-stage,* ROBINSON *to the right. A long silence.*

SMITH: How long?

ROBERTSON: As long as it takes. He's doing a cell check. Mr Fairbrass likes everything correct. He'll start on the top landing and make his way down. If he finds anything unusual he'll investigate. So stand still and be quiet. (*Pause.*) Ah. There you are, Mr Fairbrass.

FAIRBRASS: Here I am indeed, Mr Robertson.

He comes up behind SMITH. SMITH *goes to turn.*

No one told you to turn!

ROBERTSON: No one told you to turn, Smith!

FAIRBRASS *inspects* SMITH *from behind.*

I think this one's sick all right. Does peculiar things with Bibles. Goes on about God all the time. Been talking about all sorts of nonsense. Definitely a head job.

FAIRBRASS: We'll let the doctor decide that. That's his job. We're custodians, not psychiatrists.

ROBERTSON: Right then, Mr Fairbrass. I'm late as it is. I'll go. His name's Smith. John William Smith. And the doctor wants to see him tomorrow. I'll say goodnight . . . I was hoping to go to the pictures . . .

FAIRBRASS (*still behind* SMITH): Prefer you to stay Mr Robertson. While I check this man. You know what these . . . ethnics are like.

SMITH *goes to turn.* FAIRBRASS *forces his face forward.*

Keep your eyes *that* way. When you can't see the enemy, *Smith*, that puts you at a distinct disadvantage. Because I am the enemy, have no fear on that score. By the time you leave here, you won't want to come back in a hurry. I don't like to see the same faces coming back time and time again. I feel as though I've failed. D'you understand that? Don't answer! It's a question for you to think about. (*Pause.*) Know him Mr Robertson, do you? A regular, is he? Hard to tell with black faces. . .

ROBERTSON: I've never seen this one before. He's harmless, I'd say. Wears poofy clothes and I think he thinks he's in touch with God. But he did head-butt a PC. Don't know how true that is . . .

FAIRBRASS: If that was on the charge-sheet, Mr Robertson, *that* is what happened. It's not for you to question the law. If we can't believe the law, what can we believe? (*Pause.*) Now, we'll have roll-call. When I call your name I want a clear and precise 'Yes sir'! Understood? (*Pause.*) Smith!

SMITH *goes to turn.* ROBERTSON *gestures a warning.*

SMITH: Sir.

FAIRBRASS: Smith!

SMITH: Yes, sir.

FAIRBRASS (*menacing*) Don't fuck about with me. Smith!

SMITH: Yes, sir!

FAIRBRASS (*pause*): Jesus! (*Long pause.*) So. You can't win in here, mate. Don't try me. Ever. Not even in thought. (*Pause.*) Let's get things clear from the start. For your information, this is a prison, not a hospital. Right, Mr Robertson?

ROBERTSON (*he's heard it before*): A prison, Mr Fairbrass . . . (*He looks at his watch.*)

FAIRBRASS (*paces behind* SMITH): And this wing is where you come when you get remanded in custody for a medical report. You come to this wing, in a prison. So you're not a special case, anything like that. (*He stops behind* SMITH.) You are here because the bench you have appeared before couldn't determine the state of your mind. (*Pause.*) They haven't our experience, have they Mr Robertson?

ROBERTSON: That's about —

FAIRBRASS: Be that as it may, you can rest assured that in this establishment there is no confusion on that little score. In here, you are nothing but a name and number. Like the other four thousand or so cons who are as yet untried, in here, and various other custodial palaces. That is a fact. Whether you're mad, guilty or just plain ugly doesn't come into it. (*He begins pacing.*) We are not interested in individuals.

ROBERTSON *looks at his watch.*

In other words, your only status whilst you are in prison is that of a prisoner, a con. And the same rules apply in this wing as in any other wing in the prison. Right? (*Pause.*) Mr Robertson, you can bang this man up for the night. Read him the riot act in the meanwhile. Tell him how cross I get if he isn't out of his cell quickly in the morning to slop out. Tell him we have a different set of rule books than the ones gathering dust on the shelves at the Home Office. And tell him that I will not stand any nonsense on questions of a racial nature. In here, it's dog eat dog. *Tough* if you can't defend yourself. (*Pause.*) And lastly, Mr Robertson, tell him that my temper is *mild*, compared to Mr Wood's! Put the black bastard away! Ground two. A windowless cell for a violent con. Look lively then Mr Robertson! You'll be late for the pictures!

SMITH *turns to look at* FAIRBRASS. FAIRBRASS *turns his back on* SMITH.

ROBERTSON: Move it, Smith! That way!

Lights down.

Scene Six

A cell. A square of light on SMITH. *He sits on the floor, very still, his hands clasped in prayer.*

Pause.

The sound of lights being switched off, faint then loud. Ten sounds. The square of light off of SMITH.

SMITH (*a frantic whisper*): Oh, God . . . oh my sweet Jesus, help me . . . Don't leave me in darkness. I'm afraid . . . I'm afraid . . . Can you see your child in the darkness? He's fearful of the night . . . My knuckles are white with fear . . . My nails cut into my palms in terror . . . Hands are around my throat . . . I feel a cold breath on my face . . . The coldness of the dead is wrapping itself around me . . . I'm afraid, Lord . . . Are you there? Speak to me . . . speak to me from the darkness . . . Let your love fill the dark . . . Oh, Jesus . . . Jesus . . . (*Hard.*) Jesus! Where have you gone! Why have you left me?

In the darkness SMITH *begins to hammer on the door, about six times.*

Silence.

Scene Seven.

The DOCTOR'*s surgery. The* DOCTOR *sits on a chair.* SMITH *stands before the* DOCTOR. *He hangs his head in tired resignation.*

DOCTOR (*pause*): What have you got to say for yourself. Smith?

SMITH (*looking slowly up*): I queued up this morning with a parcel of shit. Streams of men carrying their parcels of shit. Black men and white men trying to pretend they were alone . . . emptying their parcels of shit.

DOCTOR (*pause*): It's . . . the usual practice. It's called slopping out.

SMITH: A man told a joke. We stopped to listen. No one laughed. The man who told the joke started crying. Such humiliation, not to get a laugh at a good joke . . .

DOCTOR: Tell me something about yourself, Smith. Forget about . . . your surroundings.

SMITH: God has left the world. He's turned away in disgust. He left me in darkness last night. (*Pause.*) Mr F has replaced him . . . He's a carnivorous monster. He'll eat us all. He had the worm inside him. Forever hungry. Forever and ever, Amen. (*Pause.*) What do you want to know? I'm a black man living in a white world with a black soul. I used to live in Hackney. (*Pause.*) Once . . .

DOCTOR: Did you work?

SMITH: With clothes. Without people in them. I like clothes.

DOCTOR: Married?

SMITH: I kept strictly to dresses.

DOCTOR: D'you have a job?

SMITH: I'm sick, man

DOCTOR: Sick?

SMITH: My body's sick. All through me.

DOCTOR (*reads*): What was the idea of the Bible on your back, may I ask?

SMITH: The word of God, man.

DOCTOR: I know what the Bible contains. But what were you doing with a Bible on your back in a busy main road . . . causing a traffic jam?

SMITH: I don't know . . . Not guilty.

DOCTOR (*pause*): And whilst you were being arrested you assaulted a policeman. Butted him with your head. You caused a great deal of distress to an officer of the law: he has a broken nose.

SMITH: Which one? There were so many . . . Arms and legs . . . And sticks . . . And ugly, savage faces screaming at me . . . Suddenly the light went out. I became afraid. The darkness cripples me, Doctor. The light went out in there. (*Points.*) And I froze. I couldn't talk to God. I couldn't see. I was blinded by the dark.

DOCTOR (*pause*): Why are you afraid of the dark?

SMITH: The darkness covers the sins of the world.

DOCTOR (*slight anger*): Yes, but why are you afraid of the dark? You're not a child. You're a grown man.

SMITH: When I was a child I hated going to bed. (*Pause.*) Bed . . . darkness . . . night noises . . . breath. Breathing The smell of whisky. Breathing. Grass. Sucking . . . breathing.

DOCTOR: Your own?

SMITH: Others.

DOCTOR: What others? People sharing the same room? Your brothers and sisters? Your parents? Who?

SMITH (*pause*): Sometimes the street light still came through a chink in the curtains. I knew I had to wait until it went away. Until someone took the light away from out there. They moved it on. Somewhere. Into the shadows.

DOCTOR (*pause*): Who were you sharing a room with? Were you ever in borstal?

SMITH (*pause*): They didn't always wait. Once a train passed at the back of the house. Then a cat screamed; a dustbin lid rattled. Broken glass. A distant cry . . . A going away . . .

DOCTOR: *Who* didn't always wait?

SMITH (*long pause*): You know. You're as old as they are. You went to the same school. Ate the same school meals . . . learnt the same fucking lessons . . .

DOCTOR: Smith, believe me, I don't know who you mean. I don't know these people you're referring to. I need you to tell me. (*Pause.*) Please tell me.

SMITH (*pause*): They. And they still go to church! To church . . . All that fucking jive. Then he drives the big red bus around London like he was the Lord Mayor.

DOCTOR: I'd like you to refrain from bad language, Smith. D'you understand?

SMITH (*nods*): Silence. Answer the questions.

DOCTOR: That's better. (*Pause.*) So when it . . . became dark, what happened then? What did *they* do?

SMITH: They preached one thing but did another. (*Pause.*) They said, there's the commandments for *you* . . . We have our own. At the front of the house, outside, late at night, people were hurrying past the lower window. Sometimes the wind would carry the music to me. Sweet, man . . .

DOCTOR: You haven't told me what *they* did. Did *they* frighten you?

SMITH: Oh, yes. I made a new darkness by closing my eyes. But the darkness spoke in my ears. I could hear the darkness. It said everything. It knew everything.

DOCTOR: Tell me. Tell me, Smith.

SMITH (*long pause*): What the darkness said?

DOCTOR: Yes.

SMITH: Everything?

DOCTOR: Yes.

SMITH (*pause*): Breath. Breath. Breathing. (*Pause.*) They fucked violently in the darkness beside me! Right there beside me, man! In the same room! (*Pause.*) He murdered her. I was a witness in the dark; playing with my own cock . . .

DOCTOR (*long pause*): I see . . .

SMITH: Devastation, man . . .

DOCTOR: Yes . . .

SMITH: Gods knows I suffered that night . . . And all the other nights of my life. He knows.

DOCTOR: *He* gives you comfort, does he?

SMITH: Who is there to listen? Nobody listens.

DOCTOR: No.

SMITH: Everyone's screaming. Silently.

DOCTOR: Yes . . .

SMITH: Do you know where God has gone?

DOCTOR (*pause*): Has *He* gone?

SMITH (*long pause*): He's not here.

DOCTOR: Perhaps . . . Tell me, Smith, do you take drugs? Did you take drugs?

SMITH: I went through the card. They don't reach me . . . They don't touch me . . . Life is a drug.

DOCTOR (*pause*): I see . . . Yes . . .

SMITH: I'm afraid of that man.

DOCTOR: Who? (*Pause.*) Your father?

SMITH: I'm not afraid of ghosts. No, *him*, the man who stands behind you out there.

DOCTOR: The officer?

SMITH: He's mean.

DOCTOR: Which officer do you mean? The one I saw you with last night?

SMITH: No. The other one. Pure evil. Like a cancer. He's waiting to crawl into my gut.

DOCTOR (*pause*): You mean Mr Fairbrass.

SMITH: You know . . .

DOCTOR: Yes . . . Unfortunately, there's a Fairbrass in every corner of life. His kind are also part of the picture . . . I'm sorry . . .

SMITH: I think he wants to harm me. He's the devil's man.

DOCTOR: You mustn't be afraid. No harm will come to you in here. I'll see to that. Promise.

SMITH: And will you keep the light on?

DOCTOR: What do you mean?

SMITH: In my space. I can't pray without seeing. Not anymore . . .

DOCTOR (*pause*): I'll arrange to have the light kept on in your cell. (*Pause.*) How will you sleep? Isn't it difficult with the light on all the time?

SMITH: I sleep awake.

DOCTOR: Oh . . . Tell me, do you pray *all* the time?

SMITH: All the time.

DOCTOR: Do you pray for anything . . . special?

SMITH: Yeah.

DOCTOR: What?

SMITH: Strength.

DOCTOR: Strength for what?

SMITH: To continue breathing, man. To stay with it . . . Or to get out of it . . . One way or the other.

DOCTOR (*pause*): Do you ever think of . . . getting out of it all?

SMITH: Out of here?

DOCTOR: No. Out of life. D'you ever

think of ending your life? (*Long
pause.*) Did you hear what I said?

SMITH (*upset*): Strength to live . . .

DOCTOR: I'm sorry. I didn't want to
upset you. But I have to ask . . .
certain questions . . . You will
appreciate that, Smith. Believe it or
not, it's for your own good.

SMITH: The world's turning bad. We've
lost love. You can't live a life without
that. It can overcome armies of hate.
It can turn the meanest eye. Right,
man?

DOCTOR: Can you love Mr Fairbrass?

Pause. The DOCTOR *is amused.*

You sound . . . hopeful at least . . . (*He
stands.*) But I think that will be all for
today. I see you have to go back to
court in three weeks time. I'll try and
see you once more before then.

SMITH: Back to my space.

DOCTOR: Back to your space. I'm going
to prescribe tranquillisers for you. Ease
your mind a little. Help you to relax.
Help you to carry on . . . They'll be
given to you at night.

SMITH: I'll sing for you.

DOCTOR: That's very nice of you.

SMITH: My father said in Jamaica he
sang all the time . . .

DOCTOR: We aren't in Jamaica now! I'm
afraid you have to go back to your
cell.

SMITH (*hurt*): Yes, sir . . .

DOCTOR (*calls*): Officer!

FAIRBRASS *enters.*

FAIRBRASS: You called, Doctor.

DOCTOR (*not looking at* FAIRBRASS):
This man can go back to his cell. I've
prescribed tranquillisers for him and I
want his cell light left on at all times.
Is that understood?

FAIRBRASS: Right. Tranquillisers and a
light to be left on at all times. Move,
Smith!

FAIRBRASS *and* SMITH *move off.*
The DOCTOR *sits. He starts shaking.*
Lights down.

Scene Eight

SMITH's *cell.* SMITH *and* FAIRBRASS.

FAIRBRASS (*staring at* SMITH's *back*):
Tranquillisers eh? And the light left
on. Go around like a zombie, eh? You
won't even know you're in the nick
will you? Won't feel a bloody thing!
And nine months' time you'll be back
again.

SMITH: I'm afraid of the dark.

FAIRBRASS: Are you now? What a pity.
What a terrible thing. Afraid the
bogeyman'll get you, eh? Afraid
someone might leave your cell door
open and let a couple of nasties in to
. . . rough you up? Hm? You lying
bastard! Afraid of the darkness my
arse! Sympathy off that idiot of a
doctor, that's what you're after.
Looking for the easy way out. Not
while I've got breath in my body, mate.
I can see through you as clear as day.

SMITH: I never lie. You would know. I
can't lie.

FAIRBRASS: You're dead right.

SMITH: Yes . . .

FAIRBRASS: You might be able to pull
the wool over the doctor's eyes, but
not mine. I've been too long in the
game. Too long amongst you miserable
animals. So don't try and come it with
an old soldier, mate. Or you'll be for
it. And let's get one more thing
straight. I don't like blacks. And in
particular I don't like black men who
cause injury to PCs or members of Her
Majesty's Prison Service. Have you
understood? And you can't hide
behind your madness from *this* bloke.
I'm an expert on human nature. The
doctor lives in a retreat half the time.
What does he know? Words on a menu

ain't the same thing as eating the meal. Ha. What do any of them know, or care come to that, sitting at their polished desks two million miles away? They think we've got endless space the way they keep packing you in.

SMITH: Packed in like sardines . . . little fishes . . .

FAIRBRASS: Shut up!

SMITH (*goes to turn, stops*): Silence . . .

FAIRBRASS: You just remember that.

SMITH: I can see you.

FAIRBRASS: Eh?

SMITH: I heard your voice, man, and I see you in my mind. Silly man. Silly little six-foot fascist man with no cock. Rar rar rar . . . Amen.

FAIRBRASS: What did you say?

SMITH: Amen.

FAIRBRASS (*pause*): I'll destroy you.

SMITH: God won't let you. He protects his children.

FAIRBRASS: Whatever way you leave here, rest assured it won't be the same way you entered.

SMITH: Throw me to the lions. My ancestors were thrown to the lions . . . but they survived . . . Now they roar like the lion. God is power!

FAIRBRASS: I'm going to enjoy this. Do you honestly think you can provoke me and get away with it? You aren't provoking Old Bill now you know. There's no running in here. There's no racial discrimination board in here, you black fucker! There's no place for you to go. I'll nail you to the wall. You're dead.

SMITH (*pause*): Yes . . . yes. I'm dead. It's better to be dead in a heap of shit. It's the only way, man. Living alive in it is bad news . . .

FAIRBRASS (*looks either way*): Move forward, Smith! You get in that corner and strip. I've got my suspicions about you. I think you're concealing dangerous drugs. So off with your clothes! Be quick!

SMITH: These are not my clothes. I've nothing.

FAIRBRASS: That's what we're going to find out. Take them off! And place them in a neat pile! I dislike sloppiness. And keep your bloody face to the wall.

SMITH *slowly takes his clothes off; they should form a neat pile. He stands naked and still.*

SMITH: Born again . . . Born again . . .

FAIRBRASS: Move forward. Further. Face the wall. Get up to it!

SMITH: The Lord is my shepherd . . .

FAIRBRASS: Shut up!

He moves to the pile of clothes. He stands over them. He urinates over them.

ROBINSON *enters during the action of* FAIRBRASS. *Pause. He is shocked.*
ROBERTSON: Mr Fairbrass?

FAIRBRASS (*without looking*): Don't interrupt me, Mr Robertson. Can't you see I'm busy?

ROBERTSON, *disgusted, leaves hurriedly.*

FAIRBRASS *finishes. Pause. He stands back.*

This time you were lucky, Smith. I didn't find anything. (*Pause.*) Get dressed.

A long pause. SMITH *slowly dresses, very distressed.*

I know you're capable of concealing something. Because you're a cute one. It seems to me that the safest thing I can do is to make periodic searches. Of your clothes . . . And of your person. The body does have hiding places, doesn't it? Do you understand? You're potentially a very bad man, Smith.

SMITH: I'm not bad.

FAIRBRASS: I say you are. I say you're bad.

SMITH (*still dressing*): 'Who are you to pass judgement on the servant of another . . . It is before his own master that he stands or falls . . . And he will be upheld, for the master is able to make him stand . . .' (*He finishes dressing. He turns.*)

FAIRBRASS: What are you mumbling about?

SMITH (*pause*): Romans 14.

FAIRBRASS: I'm your master, mate. In here I'm the master. Don't forget it. There are two sets of rules in any system. The rules that are written and the rules of action. In here we opt for the latter. It's a question of expediency. When you throw all different sorts of meat into the stew-pot, it's very difficult to determine what the end result will turn out like. (*Pause.*) Lights out! (*He moves back.*) I'll let the doctor know you're back safe and secure in your pad. I'll be seeing you again very soon. (*He moves back.*)

Lights off on SMITH. *Banging, six times.*

FAIRBRASS *pauses, then leaves, bracing himself.*

Lights down.

Scene Nine

The prison wing. Enough light to see. A sobbing is heard.

ROBERTSON (*comes across the stage*): Is that you crying, Smith? (*Pause.*) I said is that you crying, Smith? Don't you like the darkness? (*Pause.*) I'll put the cell light on . . . There! (*Pause.*) Didn't make the pictures after all . . . Try and go tomorrow . . . My missus'll be very upset . . .

Square of light on SMITH. *He is huddled in a corner.*

(*As though talking through a door.*) I

mean, mate, don't judge us all alike. I mean, don't . . . make swine out of all of us. And think of the conditions we have to work in. There ain't enough of us to do the job properly. And even if there were, there ain't the space. What spaces there are, are like kegs of dynamite. They could blow any minute. (*Pause.*) Make the Brussels riot look like chicken feed . . . (*A bit louder.*) No votes in prison you see! No political kudos in improving conditions either! (*Quieter.*) No one cares a monkey's you see . . . (*Pause.*) D'you see? (*Pause.*) No, I don't suppose you do . . . Poor fucker . . . Goodnight, Smith! Goodnight.

He slowly walks off.

Lights down.

Scene Ten

The surgery. The DOCTOR *in a square of light. He sits on a chair. He drinks from a hip flask.*

FAIRBRASS *comes quickly on stage.*

He catches the DOCTOR *drinking. Pause. A sly grin.*

FAIRBRASS: Ah . . .

DOCTOR (*looks up quickly*): Yes?

FAIRBRASS: Just taking your night-cap I see . . . I won't disturb you. What I have to say can wait . . . Nothing important. (*He slowly walks off.*)

The DOCTOR *looks after him, anger mixed with powerlessness.*

Cut lights quickly.

ACT TWO

Scene One

The prison wing. SMITH *praying, left.* FAIRBRASS *stands rigid, right. The* DOCTOR *enters from the rear, followed by* ROBERTSON.

DOCTOR: Good afternoon, Mr Fairbrass. (*He gestures.*) If you don't mind, I'd like to see the prisoner, Smith.

FAIRBRASS: Unusual time, doctor; four-thirty in the afternoon. Not standard practice to open cell doors at this hour. Security involved you know. Open the door on some of these men, they're liable to run riot. Something wrong, Mr Robertson? (*Pause.*) Do you know something I don't know? Has there been a complaint?

DOCTOR: Mr Robertson opened the door for me. I left my pass key in the hospital wing. It's pouring with rain. I didn't want to get wet. (*Firm.*) There's been no complaints . . .

ROBERTSON: Just escort for the doc, Mr Fairbrass. Nothing more. I'm off duty now. I'll take the doc back and away I go. Make another attempt at going to the pictures . . . Missus is climbing up the wall . . . Going to see *The Killing Fields.* I hope . . .

FAIRBRASS: So you want to see Smith?

DOCTOR: Very quickly. Just a minute or two.

FAIRBRASS: Just a minute or two, eh? Well, then, so you shall.

Pause.

FAIRBRASS (*goes to* SMITH): Smith! Outside! Be quick!

SMITH *walks to centre-stage. Pause.*

SMITH: Outside in.

DOCTOR (*pause*): It's me, Smith. The doctor.

SMITH (*pause*): It's you, the doctor. Thank you for the medication. I didn't

get it. I don't exist anymore. (*Pause.*) I'm wet.

DOCTOR: Yes, well, so am I . . . It's raining quite hard. But you should have had your medication. What happened, officer?

FAIRBRASS: You just heard the man, Doctor. He says he doesn't exist. Do you believe him or me? He had his medication last night. He's forgotten. (*He goes behind* SMITH.) You forgot, right? Remember, I dished out the pills before going off duty?

SMITH (*looks at the* DOCTOR, *at* ROBERTSON): Hard rain . . .

ROBERTSON: Pissing down. . .

FAIRBRASS: Just hold your noise while the doctor looks at you. We won't be very far away, Doctor . . . Just call if he gets out of hand . . . (*He moves back.*)

DOCTOR (*pause*): I just wanted to see how you were. Exercise your legs for a few minutes.

SMITH: Walk?

DOCTOR: Yes. Walk. Up and down. Just, just here . . .

SMITH *is puzzled. Slowly and rigidly, he paces backwards and forward.*

SMITH: Again?

DOCTOR: Again, yes. A bit of movement . . . It's very good for you . . . Good for the circulation.

SMITH *changes direction and walks towards* FAIRBRASS.

FAIRBRASS: Don't come any closer.

SMITH *stops. Pause.*

DOCTOR: Keep this end, Smith.

ROBERTSON (*pointing at his watch*): I say, Doctor, it's er, getting late . . .

DOCTOR: Just two minutes . . .

FAIRBRASS: Don't be so impatient Mr Robertson. The prisoner needs a bit of exercise after all that praying . . .

SMITH *is now walking a circle between the three.*

SMITH: So ... So this is the trick of the little boxes ... Don't tell me what's inside ... Let me open them ... Ah! (*Pause.*) Another box ... Don't tell me ... Ah! (*Pause.*) Another box. No, don't tell me! Another fucking box! And another! Fucking boxes everywhere! And they are all empty! Nothing! (*Wild.*)

FAIRBRASS *and* ROBERTSON *draw their sticks.*

DOCTOR: Smith! Get back into the cell! Now! Or you'll regret it! Now! Right now! (*He calms.*) Go into your cell and I promise no harm will come to you. Please do as I say. I'll arrange for you to have a sedative. I'll bring it myself. Please go into your cell. (*Holding his hand up to the officers.*) Go on ... in you go. There's a good man.

SMITH *pauses, calms down.*

There is a loud clap of thunder.

Silence.

SMITH: 'Our Father who art in Heaven, hallowed be thy name ... Thy Kingdom come ...' (*He stands at the cell door and looks in.*) 'For ever and ever ... Amen.' (*He goes into the cell.*)

The DOCTOR, FAIRBRASS *and* ROBERTSON *go to the cell door. They stare in at* SMITH.

SMITH *tries to strangle himself with his hands. He calms down and sits on the floor.*

No love, no wife, no future ... no life ... And God is in the clock tower. (*To the* DOCTOR.) I am something to be looked at. You see me now, walking the perimeter fence of the white moon. I'm looking for a gate. If I can find the gate, I'll push it open and go in. There were no signs, man. No 'beware of the dog'. Things like that. Just miles and miles of fence, stretching into the abyss of time. Such a journey ... It weakened me. I stopped on the way. Resting. Tired from my travels. And I looked for God on the surface of the moon. (*Pause.*) He wasn't there, where I had just come from. So he had to be where I was just going. It made some sort of sense ... (*He points to his head.*) Up here, in this time capsule. (*Pause.*) Are you the three wise men looking for God? He went that way ... (*He points down.*) your man. My man, he's that way ... (*He points up and all around.*) And all ways, in every direction ... Like pips in a jar of strawberry jam. And just as sweet ... I'm hopeful ... *You* haven't a dog's chance in hell of finding anything. Not in the direction you're heading. I am on the road to Damascus. And you are in shit street. Let us pray ... fuck fuck fuck fuck fuck ... Amen. (*He is still and silent.*)

FAIRBRASS (*moving away*): Filth ... It wouldn't be medication I'd give him ...

He puts his stick away. The DOCTOR *and* ROBERTSON *move away from the cell.* ROBERTSON *puts his stick away.*

DOCTOR: We *must* keep a close watch on him all the same. He's in grave danger from himself. (*He looks hard at* FAIRBRASS.)

ROBERTSON: Excuse me, Doctor, but I'll be late for the pictures again if I'm not careful. It's the first time me and the wife's been out for months. You understand?

DOCTOR: Oh, yes ... Sorry to have kept you.

FAIRBRASS: A bad habit to get into, Doctor, all the same ... Forgetting your keys. A grave security risk if nothing else ...

He looks at ROBERTSON

DOCTOR: Yes, very stupid of me. Very stupid ... I take it you'll do what's necessary, Mr Fairbrass. I will call back later myself. With the keys.

FAIRBRASS: What do you mean, Doctor? The *necessary?*

DOCTOR: Well, more . . . surveillance. More periodic cell checks. Remove his . . . boot laces. Things like that. He might . . . injure himself. He's very disturbed.

FAIRBRASS: Naturally, Doctor. As per the rule book. And of course you can always drop by to see that the rules are being observed, can't you? Which, I might add, are extremely difficult to adhere to with the present shortage of staff. But like I say, you're always free to come across yourself . . . Unless of course you've got something better to do. Like Mr Robertson here, who suddenly developed a passion for the movies . . . Did you have anything planned for tonight, Doctor?

DOCTOR: Well, well, actually . . . I, er, did. Yes.

FAIRBRASS: Well isn't that jolly? Bit of a cocktail party, eh? Theatre, maybe. Or is it the opera? Maybe it's an up-town restaurant. Perhaps a night in with the telly, eh; with the dinner tray on your lap? (*Pause.*) Enjoy whatever you do, Doctor. Things at this end will go on as before. No fear of that. Well, I can almost hear your sigh of relief.

DOCTOR: I'm naturally worried about Smith. I need . . . assurances . . .

FAIRBRASS: Oh, yes. Naturally. (*Pause.*) You have my assurance. But of course, human beings aren't perfect, are they? Human assurances are fallible, as you no doubt have already observed. But the intention is quite genuine . . . Doctor. We all *mean* well, most of the time. But there are grey areas to be reckoned with.

DOCTOR: And the black.

FAIRBRASS: An intended pun, Doctor? Very good.

DOCTOR: No pun intended.

FAIRBRASS: Mr Robertson will be late for the pictures.

DOCTOR: I'll come back to see Smith later. I do have rather an urgent appointment this evening . . . a seminar . . .

FAIRBRASS: Yes, I'm sure you do. Good day, Doctor. And enjoy the film this evening, Mr Robertson.

ROBERTSON: Oh, I will. The missus is very excited at the prospect. She always gets excited going up west. Well, Mr Fairbrass. Have a . . . peaceful rest of the day . . .

ROBINSON *and the* DOCTOR *leave.*

FAIRBRASS *goes to the cell. He looks in. Light is on* SMITH. FAIRBRASS *turns the light out by gesture. Darkness on* SMITH. *A muffled banging is heard.* FAIRBRASS *raises his hand, the light comes on.* SMITH *is standing at the door. He appears to be holding something. The banging stops the moment the light comes on.* FAIRBRASS *repeats the action. Finally he leaves the light off. The banging continues. He moves away.*

ROBERTSON (*comes back hurriedly*): I'll be late for my own funeral . . . Almost forgot, Mr Fairbrass. What shift am I on tomorrow?

FAIRBRASS (*pause*): Early, Mr Robertson. Bright and early.

ROBERTSON: Well I'm on a promise tonight, but I'll try and make it . . . What's that?

FAIRBRASS: What's what?

ROBERTSON: That noise. A banging noise. I do believe it's coming from Smith's cell. What happens, Mr Fairbrass, is that when the light isn't on, Smith gets the horrors and canes the door with the washstand. You know? Night officer mentioned it . . .

FAIRBRASS: Does he now? Well when he breaks the washstand he won't be able to do it, will he? Bright and early, Mr Robertson.

ROBERTSON: Bright and early . . . (*He goes to the cell.*) Must have switched the light off by mistake. Doctor'll be giving me a right telling off, forgetting to keep the light on . . . at all times. (*He switches the light on by gesture. The banging stops.*) There. Works wonders. You wouldn't want to be listening to that noise all evening, sir, would you? (*Leaving.*) Goodnight once more . . .

He goes but stays in the background

FAIRBRASS (*moves to the cell. Pause. He draws his stick and steps into the cell.*) Step back! (*Pause.*) I think you're hiding something from me. Get your clothes off, boy. Put them in a neat pile beside you. And face the wall I don't want to look at your black prick. Move it!

SMITH slowly undresses and piles his clothes neatly. He stands naked. Pause.

SMITH: Sinner, you can't reach me.

FAIRBRASS (*pause*): Scum. You can't hide in here. Go on. Try.

SMITH: 'In the Lord I take refuge; how can you say to me, 'Flee like a bird to the mountains''; for lo, the wicked bend the bow, they have fitted their arrow to the string, to shoot in the dark at the upright in heart; if the foundations are destroyed, what can the righteous do?' (*Pause.*) Piss and be damned! Unfairbrass!

FAIRBRASS moves swiftly and gives SMITH two blows to the back. SMITH drops to the floor.

FAIRBRASS: Wrong trick, Smith!

ROBERTSON *leaves quietly.*

SMITH (*lying on the floor*): You pig . . .

FAIRBRASS: Two sharp blows in the kidney region. Very effective. Very discreet. You'd better start behaving yourself, boy. I want some co-operation from you. Some respect. I want respect to be oozing out of your eyes and the pores of your body.

I want to feel it. If not . . . Oh, by the way, time for introductions. Look up at me, Smith!

SMITH *raises his face.*

That's better. (*He puts his stick under SMITH's chin.*) This is Mr Wood. (*He waves the stick.*) I did warn you, didn't I? (*Pause.*) I'll leave the light on a bit. As an inducement . . . Let's see how that works out . . .

He moves slowly out of the cell. He stop

Lights down quickly.

Scene Two

The prison wing. Late evening. A storm is heard. FAIRBRASS stands rigid at stage right. SMITH is in the cell. SMITH sits on the floor tearing his shirt into strips very methodically. He joins the pieces together to make them longer. When he has three long lengths he begins to plait them into one strong piece.

FAIRBRASS *does a cell-check around the perimeter of the stage, sometimes peering through spy-holes, sometimes staring through windowed doors. He reaches SMITH's cell and looks in.*

FAIRBRASS: So. This is how you repay my generous nature, eh? Damaging prison property. What a show of gratitude, eh? You're a bad man. So from now on, you'll have to rip your clothes up in the dark, won't you? (*Pause.*) I can't imagine why you should want to do such a thing . . . Looks like you're making a bit of a rope . . . Tie up a prison officer. Something evil no doubt . . . Well we mustn't make it easy for you. Perhaps you'll tie yourself in a knot with the light off . . . (*Pause.*) Haven't you got nothing to say to me?

SMITH *totally ignores him.*

Pause. FAIRBRASS steps back. Light off on SMITH. FAIRBRASS goes stage-right; waits for banging. He gets angry at the silence.

Slow lights.

Scene Three

Outside the prison. Late evening. The
DOCTOR *and* MR ROBINSON *meet by*
accident. The DOCTOR *is in a dinner*
suit, MR ROBERTSON *in uniform. The*
DOCTOR *is under the influence.*

DOCTOR: Oh, good evening, Mr
Robertson. I thought you were at the
pictures.

ROBERTSON: Yes, I was. A very good
film. Wife enjoyed it as well. She
enjoyed John Lennon's singing at the
end. Made her cry.

DOCTOR: I'm glad to hear you both
enjoyed it. What are you doing back at
the prison? You're not on night-work,
are you?

ROBERTSON: I might ask you the same
thing, Doctor. You're not exactly
dressed for an official visit, are you?
What would the cons think, seeing
you dressed like that?

DOCTOR: I wonder . . . No, well, I was
rather worried about that man, Smith.
He . . . worries me. But what are you
here for?

ROBERTSON: Just arrived home with
our Chinese take-away and the
telephone rings. Two night-shift men
have gone sick. Would I mind going in,
they said. Anyway, I'd taken the
missus to the pictures so that
simplified matters. I said I would come
in for half a shift. Mr Fairbrass is doing
the other half. He won't like that. He's
a bit of an irritation even when he's
working normal shifts. Part of the
reason I've come a little earlier . . .
Gets me down his moaning . . . There
are times when I can just about keep
my hands off of him . . .

DOCTOR: Yes, he is a bit of a . . .

ROBERTSON: He's been a prison officer
for many years. Was in the army
before that. A man of experience. Did

he ever show you the scar on his neck?
A real nasty one. He was working in
Parkhurst in 1969 during the riots. A
con tried to cut his throat. He often
talks about it in the mess, that riot.
Gets the men all worked up it does.
Very uncomfortable . . . He told us that
the man who attacked him was one of
the main leaders of the riot. A real nasty
number by all accounts. An armed
robbery man. Fairbrass always causes a
laugh when he says the con won't be
waving any more shotguns about —
because he don't know the difference
between a shotgun and a bow and
arrow these days!

DOCTOR: D'you laugh with the rest of
the men?

ROBERTSON: No. No. I don't laugh.

DOCTOR: Neither would I.

ROBERTSON: The con was bang out of
order though. You've got to admit
that. You can't go cutting people's
throats and hope to get away with it.

DOCTOR: Have you ever had an attempt
on your life, Mr Robertson? Has a
prisoner ever attacked you?

ROBERTSON: Not me, Doctor. I've been
very lucky. Some nasty pieces of work
pass through this establishment. And I
can't say I pity these filthy bastards
who harm or molest children, crimes
of that nature. They turn my stomach.
They bring out the very devil in me all
right. Even the cons won't have any
truck with them.

DOCTOR: Ah . . . Feeding the great
myth about criminals drawing the line
when it came to crimes against
children . . .

ROBERTSON: What do you mean,
Doctor? That's a fact. I've seen some
nasty accidents where those sort of
men are concerned.

DOCTOR: But don't you see? If a man or
woman walked down the high street
with a sign on their back saying, 'I've
committed a crime against a child',

why, members of the public would devour them like a pack of wolves. And so prisoners aren't different in that respect. Just that, inside, it's more obvious. The crime and the criminal is known.

ROBERTSON: I'll say this for you, Doc; if you don't mind the abbreviation; I'm amazed you're still sane after dealing with the loonys that have passed through this nick over the years. Don't know how you've kept your head in one piece.

DOCTOR (*pause*): I'm not sure that I have . . .

ROBERTSON: You must have a strong constitution. My missus says I've got a strong constitution.

DOCTOR (*pause*): I've no way of knowing these days. You weren't at this prison when I lost my wife, were you?

ROBERTSON: Oh, sorry . . . No, I wasn't.

DOCTOR: Hit and run driver.

ROBERTSON: That's terrible.

DOCTOR: More terrible still is that my daughter was killed also.

ROBERTSON: Oh . . . What can I say?

DOCTOR: Eight years of age . . . A beautiful young . . . The bottom of my world fell out . . .

ROBERTSON: I don't suppose they ever . . . caught the driver?

DOCTOR: No.

ROBERTSON: Catching the driver would have been a little compensation I suppose. Being denied even that wasn't very nice for you. Drunken drivers should be banned for life!

DOCTOR: Yes . . . banned for life. (*He looks at his car keys.*) They were on their way to the cinema, you know . . . Fancy that, eh. With you just talking about the pictures as well.

ROBERTSON: Wish I hadn't have mentioned it in the first place . . .

DOCTOR: Oh, don't be foolish. Time, hopefully, Mr Robertson will prove to be the great healer they say it is. Time . . . Strange you know . . . but you don't *really* appreciate anyone until you lose them. Do you have any children, Mr Robertson?

ROBERTSON: Afraid not. Missus is all right. It's me. Still we have each other.

DOCTOR: Did you ever think of adopting a child?

ROBERTSON: Oh, we thought about it. We even thought about fostering. In fact we thought about it a great deal over the years. You know, all those children in care, in need of parents . . . Somehow we never got around to it.

DOCTOR: Pity.

ROBERTSON: Yes . . . Thoughts aren't enough are they? I don't think we'd bother now. It's only when you see those appeals on TV does the idea crop up again.

DOCTOR: Yes . . . I'm afraid we do seem to need constant reminders about the need to be . . . charitable. Doesn't appear to be a permanent feature in the modern world. Pity. Giving is so much like . . . receiving.

ROBERTSON: You didn't tell me what you were doing here, Doctor.

DOCTOR: Ah, yes. I wanted to look in on Smith. I promised him some medication. I forgot earlier on. I was . . . already late for my . . . dinner engagement. Some old friends . . . I . . . A celebration.

ROBERTSON: Doctor friends, eh?

DOCTOR: Doctor friends? Oh, yes, doctor friends. I'm just going to see Smith, now. I have his medication in my pocket. It's the least I can do. The least . . .

ROBERTSON: Well that's very thoughtful of you, coming back this time of night. Smith's a . . . decent bloke. I . . . er, hm.

DOCTOR: What? You were about to say something?

ROBERTSON: No. Well, yes . . . And, no.

DOCTOR: Something about Smith?

ROBERTSON: Well yes.

DOCTOR: What about him?

ROBERTSON: This is strictly off the record, you understand.

DOCTOR: Understood.

ROBERTSON: Well, it's Fairbrass and Smith.

DOCTOR: What about them?

ROBERTSON: Well they don't exactly hit it off. Mr Fairbrass, he just doesn't like blacks. He's er, inclined towards . . . Well the truth is, he's a bit of an Hitler's man. He often goes on about him in the mess. Says he had the right idea about the Jews. Says the same should happen to blacks, queers and any other rubbish living. Britain for the British he says. Very patriotic. He's a real patriot, that man. Very, very nationalistic. I mean, what I'm saying, Doctor, is, I think Smith's in trouble.

DOCTOR (pause): What else?

ROBERTSON: Something else?

DOCTOR: What else do you know about him? Is there . . . something we can pin him down with?

ROBERTSON: What do you mean?

DOCTOR: For God sake . . . Is he breaking the law! I need to know! Desperately . . .

ROBERTSON: I can't say any more (Pause.) I mean to say, Doctor, my hands are tied. Cons aren't the only ones who have ways of dealing with a grass. I've got to work with them. If you see what I mean . . .

DOCTOR: I know exactly what you mean . . .

ROBERTSON: Would you say anything under the circumstances? And I have to say this right now. If you say I've said, I'll have to deny it. Sorry about that.

DOCTOR: But if he were to go?

ROBERTSON: Don't be silly, Doctor. He'll shift to another nick, and they'd replace him with the same model. When there's a complaint, they just shift people around. If not the officers, then the cons. A right game of snakes and ladders. In the meanwhile, it wouldn't do my reputation any good. Jobs aren't all that easy to find at the moment. Although many's the time . . . Oh, well . . .

Long pause.

DOCTOR: Perhaps we should go inside now. I was enjoying the night air . . . Come . . . (They walk off.) Looks like a storm brewing . . .

Cut lights.

Scene Four

The prison wing. The storm is going on. SMITH is plaiting three strands of clothing together, slowly and methodically. We see what he is doing but not the length of the cord. FAIRBRASS is at stage-right. He stands still.

FAIRBRASS looks up as a clap of thunder is heard. He kicks his legs and begins to walk around. He looks at his watch; continues. Thunder. He reaches SMITH's cell. He looks. He turns the light off on SMITH. He moves away and takes up a position at stage-right. He looks at his watch.

ROBERTSON and the DOCTOR enter. They are both wet.

ROBERTSON (removing his hat and shaking it): Pissing down out there . . . Came all of a sudden, like . . .

FAIRBRASS: You're half an hour late! He looks at the DOCTOR.

ROBERTSON: Sorry Mr Fairbrass. Met the doctor on the way in. We got chatting. You know how it is.

DOCTOR: My fault entirely. We took cover for a minute or two . . .

FAIRBRASS: Seeing quite a bit of you lately, Doctor. Most unusual. Does that mean you'll be doing your rounds more frequently? Inspecting the food and the like . . . Busy days ahead . . .

DOCTOR: I have some medication for Smith. You will remember I said I was going to give him some. Perhaps I didn't mention it to you.

FAIRBRASS: For Smith, eh? Is he . . . special? What about the rest of the sick remands; d'you have something extra for them?

DOCTOR: It is not something extra, as you put it. But rather what I'd prescribed but forgot to administer. And the rest of the remands, as far as I can tell, are not in the immediate danger that Smith is in, in my . . . opinion. *You* saw his behaviour earlier on.

ROBERTSON: Doctor's a bit worried about Smith, Mr Fairbrass. Thinks he'll do *himself* an injury. It does happen, as you know . . .

FAIRBRASS (*pause*): It wouldn't be because he's black or anything like that, naturally.

DOCTOR: No, it wouldn't. If he were a white man I'd treat him in exactly the same way. The colour of a man's skin doesn't determine my action . . . Mr Fairbrass . . .

ROBERTSON: Bloody soaked through I am . . .

DOCTOR (*pause*): Would you open Smith's cell, please. So as I can give him his medication.

ROBERTSON: Undo my jacket I think . . . Rain's gone right through . . . (*He undoes his buttons.*)

FAIRBRASS: Smith's behaving very badly. Torn up all his clothes.

DOCTOR: That's why I want to give him medication.

ROBERTSON: Calm him down you see . . .

DOCTOR (*pause*): Well? If you don't mind . . .

Pause.

ROBERTSON: Don't trouble yourself, Mr Fairbrass, I'll open up . . . You've been on duty all day and half the night already.

FAIRBRASS: You stay where you are! I can do it. I don't think the doctor believes me. I don't think he believes me when I say Smith has been playing up. Ringing the bell. Banging on the door. But he has, hasn't he, Mr Robertson? We've both been on duty when he's played up. Right? Right Mr Robertson?

Pause.

ROBERTSON (*looks at the* DOCTOR): Well, yes, he, er, does hammer on the door . . . Although most of the doorbells are broken . . .

FAIRBRASS: There. Didn't I tell you so. As you can see, both the senior officer and the junior officer are in full agreement.

Banging from SMITH's *cell.*

DOCTOR: What's that?

FAIRBRASS: There! Proof. That's Smith. Banging at the cell door with the washstand. Couldn't have happened at a more opportune moment.

ROBERTSON (*walks slowly to the cell, looks*): Light must have been accidentally turned off . . . again. Would you believe it?

FAIRBRASS (*pause*): I turned it off to stop him ripping up the clothes. Man's practically naked. Cells are cold this time of year . . .

DOCTOR: I left definite instructions about the light! I'm extremely angry! Turn that light on immediately! How dare you contravene my orders! You're a bloody law unto yourself! It's disgraceful!

ROBERTSON (*turns the light on*): There! It's on, Doctor.

The banging stops. SMITH *has tied his boot to the end of the cord in the lighted cell. He's able to see to throw the boot over a water pipe, high in the ceiling.*

DOCTOR: I would appreciate an explanation, Mr Fairbrass. Otherwise I will be forced to take this matter further.

FAIRBRASS: Then you must do what you must do . . . In a clear and . . . steady voice. Not . . . slurred.

DOCTOR: How dare you talk to me like that!

During the following, SMITH *ties the cord around his neck and hangs himself.*

You're a menace!

FAIRBRASS: You're entitled to your opinion, Doctor. But isn't it time you were about your business? Instead of . . . calling me names in front of a junior officer . . . Which I will have to report . . . among other things. Unless it's some of these . . . *alcoholic* cons leaving empty bottles lying about! I hope you're reading me loud and clear, Doctor!

ROBERTSON: I'll open the cell door, Mr Fairbrass. No problem . . . (*He goes to the cell.*) Oh, no! We're too bloody late! Doctor!

DOCTOR (*rushes to the cell*): Oh my God . . . My God! Help me get him down . . .

ROBERTSON *removes his key chain and with a small knife cuts* SMITH *down. The* DOCTOR *works on* SMITH ROBERTSON *moves away and*

goes and faces FAIRBRASS.

FAIRBRASS (*pause*): Still sick, eh?

ROBERTSON (*pause*): No. Just still.

Pause.

FAIRBRASS *goes to the cell. He sums up what has happened. He stands between the* DOCTOR *and* ROBERTSON.

FAIRBRASS (*raising his voice*): Yes, well. One thing's for sure. He needed the light on to do that little trick. (*Pause.*) Pity about the washstand not breaking either. Cost the poor fucker his life. Shame, that. A real shame . . .

The DOCTOR *removes his coat.*

ROBERTSON *goes and stares at* FAIRBRASS.

FAIRBRASS *turns his back on* ROBERTSON.

Pause.

ROBERTSON (*screams*): My advantage Mr Fairbrass! No more! (*He strikes* FAIRBRASS *on the back of the head rendering him semi-conscious.*) You bloody animal!

DOCTOR (*stops working on* SMITH *and rushes across*): What have you done . . . Stop! For God's sake! (*He struggles with* ROBERTSON.) Stop . . .

SMITH *coughs and moves.*

DOCTOR (*turns quickly*): My God . . . My God, he's still alive . . . (*He goes to* SMITH.) You're alive!

ROBERTSON *turns.* FAIRBRASS *tries to rise . . .*

SMITH (*recovers, stands, coughs*): He is risen . . .

He looks towards FAIRBRASS *and slowly walks across to him. Pause.*

'You have heard that it was said, "An eye for an eye, a tooth for a tooth"' . . . God is just.

He begins to urinate over FAIRBRASS *as he tries to move away.*

DOCTOR (*a despairing scream*): Smith!
   Cut lights quickly.

Author's Note

*From 1981 to 1985, one hundred and
fifteen people took their own lives whilst
in custody. One was a woman. Figures for
the last three years have yet to be published.*

But the trend appears to be on the increase.

London, 1987

MADE IN SPAIN

by Tony Grounds

Characters

JACQUI
ROSY
ESTELLE
TOLLA

Scene One

The garden of a large house in north-west London. JACQUI enters. She is carrying a multitude of bags, mainly Hamleys.

JACQUI: You got to spoil 'em. That's what I say. Nice to if you can afford it. We can afford it. Thank God. I wouldn't like to be without. No, I most certainly wouldn't. Don't think I haven't had to suffer. God knows I have. I used to live in Ilford for Christ's sake. If that's not suffering, I don't know what is. I've always wanted money. Call it a fetish . . . call it what you will. I used to say to my daddy, 'If I was rich, Daddy, I'd buy a big house with a swimming pool.' And he'd say, 'If your mummy had a smeckle, she'd be your daddy, get on with your homework'. He'd eat his words if he could see me now.

ROSY enters, looking all around her, obviously impressed. She is carrying a tray of drinks.

ROSY: You got a swimming pool as well then?

JACQUI: Well no, not exactly. Not at the moment. Figure of speech. Oh, put the drinks down, love. On the table. *Sur la table.*

ROSY: You got a bit of French in you, haven't you?

JACQUI: Well, we've been a few times. Now I'll just go and give these to my little baby and I'll be straight out to fix you a drinkie. Let's get one thing straight, are you Rosy or Rosemary, what do you prefer?

ROSY: Rosy.

JACQUI: Rosy. Nice. I'm Jacqui and I want you to call me Jacqui and feel at home. None of this Jacqueline nonsense.

JACQUI takes a woollen ball on a string from one of her bags.

ROSY: Ahh!

JACQUI: Isn't that something?

ROSY: You got a little kiddie?

JACQUI: Kitten. We've got a little kitten. We've only just got her. She's so fluffy. Manny wasn't all that keen at first, but I know what to do to make him spoil me.

ROSY: What's its name?

JACQUI: Goldie. Her colouring, see.

ROSY: Nice. Am I too early by the way? My Ray just told me to get round here for dinner-time.

ROSY gasps and puts her hand over her mouth.

He didn't mean the evening dinner, did he?

JACQUI: Don't worry, darling. We'll have a lovely afternoon together. How about that? You can help me get everything ready, that'll be fun, won't it? You can start off by telling me all about yourself.

ROSY: Well, I'm Rosy but you already know that.

JACQUI goes into the house.

JACQUI: Go on, I can still hear. I'm just giving Goldie her bits. She's a month old today.

ROSY: Oh, happy birthday. Anyway. I'm 20 years old. I used to be a hairdresser. Well, I am a hairdresser really. I'm just in between appointments, as they say. Still, I'm looking around. Nice break though. All day over hot heads, you know. And I'm married to Ray. And I love him. He's lovely to me. When I'm working, he phones me up every day at the salon. And says, 'All right darling?' And I say, 'Yeah, I'm all right, Ray.' It's really embarrassing, because everyone looks and everyone's listening. He always asks me if I've made many mistakes. And generally I have. I think that's why I don't get as many appointments as the other girls. But I think one day we're going to be rich. Ray seems to be doing lots of deals at the moment. But I don't mind. He keeps saying, 'I'm going to see a man about a dog, babes.' I thought he meant it at first. I thought, 'What's he want with a dog?' I thought. Anyway my Ray's a street trader. He sells Pierre Cardin socks. Gets them off the back of a lorry and sells them cheap. Well everyone goes, 'Oh God, aint they cheap?' And they're not, see. I've got a boy and he's two years old. Ray's mum looks after him quite a lot. Got no bloody choice there. 'Oh, I'll look after him,' she goes, 'I'll look after him. Oh, aint he lovely?' I hate his mum! I really hate his mum! I think she quite likes me though, which makes me feel guilty. Anyway. Ray's lovely. He's 28. I love him. Especially in his big leather coat. He's really good-looking and all the girls look at him when he walks down the road and that. When I first saw him, I thought, I want that man. And I got him, somehow. In a disco . . . I just went up to him and went, 'Aint your hair lovely?' And touched it. He seemed to get the message. Things started from there really. He keeps saying to me, 'I'm going to buy you your own business one day, babes.' Nice innit? I love my boy. Little Ray. He can't talk at the moment but he's cuddly and got fat legs. Ray keeps saying to him, 'You're going to be a footballer one day, aren't you going to be a footballer, little Ray?' And he goes . . .

ROSY *pulls a gormless baby-face.*

He doesn't know, you see. He doesn't know what it means.

ROSY *looks around her. After a moment's thought, she nips across and lies on the sunbed. In her posh accent she calls 'waiter'. Then in mock American:*

J.R. get out of my house!

This is the life. I've always been a hairdresser. I knew when I was at school I thought, 'Oh sod this.' As far as education is concerned, see, what does it mean? O levels and those other things, those degrees and things. No. I don't think you need them. I knew when I was 14 I was going to be a hairdresser. Before that, I wanted to be a psychiatrist. Because I like the idea of a lovely wooden office. With a nice big desk, and lots of pens and that. And talking to people and saying, 'It's all right. You're a bit strained at the moment and your mind's a bit mad. But you're going to be all right, cos I'm going to look after you.' And, you know, they'd tell me all their problems and everything would be all right. But then I realised I wouldn't be able to do that cos you have to do lots and lots of studying. So I left school and got married to Ray when I was about 17. I met him when I was 14. At that disco I was telling you about. I was a virgin when I met Ray. Least that's what I told him. Don't say nuffin. You don't like to hurt their feelings. Least I don't.

JACQUI *comes out into the garden again. She has changed her clothes.*

JACQUI: I've just slipped into something a little more al fresco. Go on.

ROSY: I don't cut Ray's hair and he hates poofs.

JACQUI: Oh! Now, what do you want to drink?

ROSY: Oh, I don't mind. You choose.

JACQUI: You have what you fancy. Don't stand on ceremony with me.

ROSY: Oh, I'll have a shandy then please, ta.

JACQUI: Oh no. Have a proper drink. Have a Martini, you'll like that.

ROSY: I normally have a shandy when I go up the Castle with Ray. Unless he goes, 'I'm flush, babes.' Then I know I can have a Bacardi and coke. I love them.

JACQUI: Well try a Martini today. Now Ray's doing business with my Manny, you never know when you might be called upon to frequent somewhere a little more up-market. You better start trying to acquire the taste. Here, have an olive as well. That's the sign of true breeding. When you can eat an olive without screwing you face up. I can. Watch.

JACQUI *pops an olive in her mouth and eats it with a smile on her face.*

ROSY: Nice?

JACQUI: Horrible. But I have a position to uphold and so I'm prepared to suffer.

ROSY: Why don't you just say 'Well it's very kind of you, but I won't, thanks awfully'?

JACQUI: Here we are . . . one Martini lemonade, ice and a slice, and an olive. I want to see you drink that up and eat that up, OK?

ROSY *tentatively nibbles the olive.*

ROSY: Here, I think it's really nice. Do you think I've got natural breeding?

JACQUI *looks quite taken aback.*

No. It's all right. I'm only having a laugh. It's pigging horrid.

JACQUI: Oh good. Cheers.

They chink glasses.

ROSY: Your Manny a street trader, is he?

JACQUI *nearly chokes on her Martini.*

JACQUI: Excuse me, he's an entrepreneur.

ROSY (*sympathetically*): Oh no.

JACQUI: He makes dresses.

ROSY: Oh! Is he supplying Ray. Is that what this deal's about?

JACQUI: I don't know or wish to know about 'that side of things'. I just know the 'deal' is to be concluded today and Manny asked me to prepare a meal for the four men and their wives. By way of a celebration.

ROSY: I know it's a biggy. Cos Ray keeps going 'If this comes off, I aint never going to have to sell another pair of socks, as long as I live, babes.' Does your Manny keep mentioning the Nigerian?

JACQUI: They're coming tonight. I'm not being racist or anything, but it's so difficult to know what to give them to eat . . . you know, people from other cultures.

ROSY: Do you know why Germans are blond? Cos they eat a lot of pork.

JACQUI: Is that why Jews aren't blond?

ROSY: Do you know, you might have a point there.

JACQUI: What's blond hair got to do with pork?

ROSY: Have you ever seen those hairs on pigs? White.

JACQUI: Do you eat a lot of pork? Oh no, you're not natural are you?

ROSY: Could you tell? I did it myself.

JACQUI: How's the Martini?

ROSY: Don't say nuffin but I'm a bit tiddly. I always know when I've had too much to drink though, cos when I say something, Ray goes, 'Oh shut up you daft cow.' But we aren't half in love. I love him all the way down to to his Pierre Cardin socks. Who does your hair? Can I have a feel?

ROSY *feels JACQUI's hair.*

ROSY: Yeah. Nice.

Scene Two

A little later, in the garden. JACQUI is fast asleep on a sunbed. ROSY is watching her as she snores grotesquely. After a while ESTELLE comes into the garden. She is looking lost.

ESTELLE: Excuse me.

ROSY: Shh.

She points to JACQUI.

ESTELLE: Sorry. Is this number twenty-eight? None of the houses seem to have numbers, they've all got these poxy bloody names. 'Dun Roamin'.

ROSY: When we was on holiday, we walked past this house called 'Sea View' and there was this bloke in the garden and my husband says to him, 'Sea View Jimmy'.

ESTELLE: This must be the right house . . . you've got to be Rosy.

ROSY: That's right. How did you know?

ESTELLE: I'm a clairvoyant.

ROSY: We used to have this girl at school called Clair and we all called her clairvoyant for a laugh. But one day she hit me with her PE bag.

ESTELLE: And that has just got to be Jacqui.

ROSY: I know who you are; you're Ted's wife.

ESTELLE: Yes. I'm Ted's wife.

ROSY: Shall I wake up Jacqui?

ESTELLE: No let's let her sleep aye, poor cow.

ROSY: Your name's Estelle, isn't it?

ESTELLE: That's right, love.

ROSY: Yes. Ray's told me all about you.

ESTELLE: Has he now?

ESTELLE *picks up the Martini bottle.*
She's had a fair drop of this, has she?

ROSY: Tell you the truth, I think that's why she's dropped off.

ESTELLE: I heard she was sodden.

ROSY: I didn't like it. But I pretended I did. To be nice.
It's a lovely place they've got here, innit?

ESTELLE: More money than class.

ESTELLE *sprays some perfume behind her ears and knees.*

I'm sweating like a pig, me. If I'd've known it was that far from the bloody

tube I'd've got a cab. That's got to knock a few grand off the value of the house.

ROSY: All the dinner's on and everything's all laid up inside. Don't half look nice.

ESTELLE: Apparently she's had electrodes put behind her ears to stop her drinking. Obviously not done a lot of good.

ROSY: She's got a little cat.

ESTELLE: That's cos her old man's got a low sperm count.

ROSY: How do you count them?

ESTELLE: No. It's nothing to do with counting them. It's quality rather than quantity.

ROSY: 'Bout to say.

ESTELLE: Mind you, he's so fat, it's hardly surprising. Think I'll help myself to a little drink. Before the sponge comes round and finishes it all off.

ROSY: You've met him then, have you?

ESTELLE: Oh yeah.

ROSY: I haven't met any of the men. Apart from my Ray. And then that's hardly surprising, owing to the fact I'm married to him.

ESTELLE: Well, they've had some of the their 'meetings' round our place.

ROSY: Where's that then?

ESTELLE: Bromley. But it's nice. Well, ish.

ROSY: We're Camberwell.

ESTELLE: We've got premises in Batter . . . South Chelsea.

ROSY: What do you do then?

ESTELLE: Me? Well, I sort of deal with men's problems. Really. Along the line of physical hang-ups. I relax them. Body and mind I suppose.

ROSY: Oh?

ESTELLE: And they talk to me as well.

Which is nice. Well it can be. Yes, I work in a sort of . . .

ROSY: Parlour?

ESTELLE: Surgery. I think I'd rather call it a surgery. And it's in Chelsea. But as I say, we don't live there. We've got this three bedroomed in Bromley. Me and Ted.

ROSY: Does he have any problems?

ESTELLE: I think I've sorted most of those out. Really. He's a bit thick, but that's a problem I can't do much about.

ROSY: What does Ted do?

ESTELLE: He owns the surgery.

ROSY: Oh I see.

ESTELLE: He didn't used to. He was just a punter, but fell in love with me, so bought the surgery, so he could have me.

ROSY: That's nice.

ESTELLE: Now he wants me to stop working there, because one thing led to another with him, he assumes it's going to with everyone.

ROSY: And does it?

ESTELLE: Well Ted's an old man. But he's going to be rich. We're going to be rich. I'm going to be rich, anyway.

ROSY: So you don't tell him if anything goes on?

ESTELLE: Well, what he don't know.

ROSY: It's nice us all getting together, don't you reckon?

ESTELLE: It's obviously a big job.

ROSY: Do you know anything about it?

ESTELLE: Something in or out of Nigeria. I dunno. But it's got to make us rich.

ROSY: So my Ray reckons. He's gonna buy me a salon.

ESTELLE: You get enough money to retire, and you start work. I dunno.

Scene Three

JACQUI *is still asleep in the garden but she is now alone.* TOLLA *enters the garden.*

TOLLA: Excuse me. Hello.

TOLLA *goes over to* JACQUI *and gently shakes her sunbed.* JACQUI *wakes with a start.*

JACQUI: Oh my God, who are you?

TOLLA: I'm sorry to disturb you. Are you Jacqui?

JACQUI: Oh, you're the Nigerian.

TOLLA: Well there are others, but I'm one.

JACQUI: Oh I'm sorry, I didn't mean . . . you know.

TOLLA: Sorry to have startled you.

JACQUI: Oh no problem. You didn't. I'd just nodded off for thirty seconds. Well, I say nodded off, just thinking with my eyes closed really.

TOLLA: I'm Tolla.

JACQUI: Hello.

TOLLA: I'm not early, am I?

JACQUI: No no no no no no no. What time is it?

TOLLA: Seven-thirty. That's when my husband said to arrive. He's not here yet?

JACQUI: No. Just Rosy and myself. Rosy's Ray's wife. I expect your husband's mentioned him.

TOLLA: In passing.

JACQUI: Anyway . . . Tolla, let me fix you a drink.

JACQUI *picks up the Martini bottle and discovers it's empty. She looks quite shocked, and checks her ears to make sure the electrodes are still in place. She is relieved when she discovers that they are.*

It's all right. There's another bottle inside.

TOLLA: I'm fine thanks. Please don't bother on my account.

JACQUI: Well sit down anyhow, Tolla. Am I saying your name right? Tolla?

TOLLA: Wonderfully.

JACQUI: Oh, thanks. It's a pretty name that. Tolla. Almost French. You'd never know. I thought we'd have lamb tonight, if that's all right with you.

TOLLA: Fine.

JACQUI: Oh good. I don't know where Rosy's gone off to. Probably got herself lost in the house. I don't think she's used to big places. You should have seen her big eyes as she gazed at all my expensive artifacts. Quite taken a-back, bless her. Do you have big houses in Nigeria?

TOLLA: Well some are big, and some are small.

JACQUI: Oh, yes, of course. Sorry, I didn't mean to . . . you know.

TOLLA: I've been in England since I was five.

JACQUI: Well, you'd have got used to the weather by now then. Still, it's nice today.

TOLLA: Very pleasant.

JACQUI: Yes, Rosy and I have been sitting in the garden, chatting away. We've been getting on famously. Let me get you a drink, I'm parched.

TOLLA: Well I'll have a drop of Perrier water then please.

JACQUI: Aren't you allowed to drink?

TOLLA: I'm over eighteen.

JACQUI: Yes sorry, of course.

JACQUI *goes into the house, checking the electrodes as she goes. After a while,* ESTELLE *and* ROSY *come into the garden. They are giggling and carrying a new bottle of Martini.*

ESTELLE: Hello, love. You've got to be Tolla?

TOLLA: I'm Tolla.

ESTELLE: I'm Estelle, Ted's wife. And this is Rosy.

ROSY: Here, aint your hair nice? Who does it?

TOLLA: Me.

ROSY: Really? Ent it good? Ent it good, Estelle?

TOLLA: Thanks.

ESTELLE: She's come round then, has she, our host?

TOLLA: Jacqui? Yes, she's gone to fix a drink.

ESTELLE: That's no bloody surprise, is it?

ROSY: I do mine as well. But I don't charge myself.

TOLLA *takes an olive.*

ROSY: D'you like them?

TOLLA: Yes.

JACQUI *emerges from the house with another tray of drinks, including a huge jug of Pimms.*

JACQUI: Oh hello, all of us girls are here, I see. Now that face I don't recognise must be that of Estelle, Ted's wife. Now, I've brought out some drinks and nibbles, so we can indulge ourselves while we wait for the men. They don't know what they're missing, do they girls? I've got some Pimms Number One cup here, and some Planters, temptation beyond endurance, have you seen the advert? I only drink this because of its fruity taste. Where are the men? Let's hope they're not going to be late, the meal's almost ready. If they're not here soon we shall just have to start without them. Why are you all looking at me like that?

JACQUI *exits hurriedly, checking her electrodes as she goes.*

ROSY: Oh dear, spot of earache?

Scene Four

The dining-room of JACQUI's *house. The four women are sitting round the table. They have just finished their meal.*

ESTELLE: Well Jacqui, I must say that was bloody marvellous.

JACQUI: I just hope you were right. We haven't saved anything for the men. And Manny's got a terrible temper on him, when he's had a drink.

ESTELLE: Relax. It's their bloody fault for being three hours late. I was starving.

JACQUI: Don't get me wrong, he doesn't knock me about or anything. Really.

ESTELLE: I wish I was stronger than Ted. God I'd knock him about.

ROSY: I wouldn't really like to be stronger than Ray.

ESTELLE: Can you imagine it, eh? Being stronger than your man? It'd make all the bloody difference. 'Get up to the bedroom, get yourself . . . hard. I'm just going out to do a bit of business.'

ROSY: Actually, I think if it came to a real fight, I'd probably beat Ray, but I like to pretend he's really tough. Makes him much better. Oh when he thinks he's all powerful, he's wonderful . . . upstairs. D'you know what I mean, girls? Well, I say upstairs, we live in a flat, but you know what I'm talking about. 'How's that for you, babes?' 'Oh perfect.' 'How's that then?' 'Oh even better.'

ESTELLE: You're keeping very quiet, Tolla.

TOLLA: I'm sorry. I haven't got anything to say. That's all.

JACQUI: You're having a nice time, though?

TOLLA: I'm fine thanks.

ESTELLE: You're not worried about the men, are you? Sod 'em, that's what I say. And I'm not being hard, that's just experience talking. They get you all worried, thinking the worst, you spend hours of the night, tearing your hair out, waiting for the house to be repossessed, and the little shit comes in pissed out of his tiny head after a game of cards. They never think to bleeding ring. Yes, if I were stronger, I wouldn't half kick the shit out of Ted often.

TOLLA: It's just that I don't quite understand why they get the four of us together and then not show up themselves.

JACQUI: What do you mean 'the worst'? You said you always think the worst.

ESTELLE: Well, having their collars felt, what do you think I mean?

ROSY: You got any bubbies, Tolla?

TOLLA: No.

JACQUI: What on earth does that mean?

ROSY: Oh dear, on the pill are you?

JACQUI: Don't smirk at me, dear. I don't understand your low-life expressions.

ESTELLE: Don't play the fucking queen mother with me, dear. Your old man is as big a hood as any of our old men.

ROSY: Ent that funny, cos it was exactly the opposite with me. I wanted a bubbie, so just never took the bloody pill. Told Ray it don't work for some women.

JACQUI: My husband is a dressmaker and distributor.

ESTELLE: Fuck off.

JACQUI: How dare you use such gutter language in my home.

ESTELLE: It aint your home, it's your fat old man's, bought from the earnings of corruption.

ROSY: You must come round and see my baby sometime. He's lovely. When you see my little Ray, you're gonna want one, he's so cuddly.

JACQUI: MY HUSBAND MAKES DRESSES!

They all look at JACQUI *who is almost in tears, leans across the table and takes the bottle of wine. She pours herself a huge glass and drinks it down. She then checks behind her ears for her electrodes.*

He does. Honestly he does.

ROSY: I'm sure he does, Jacqui, don't worry yourself.

ESTELLE: It's about time she faced up to a few facts.

ROSY: Leave her, Estelle. She's a bit tiddly, that's all, aren't you, Jacqui?

JACQUI: I hardly drink.

ESTELLE: She's bloody cuckoo.

JACQUI: I'm not cuckoo.

ROSY: No, of course not.

ESTELLE: Bloody cuckoo.

JACQUI: Do you think I'm cuckoo, Tolla?

TOLLA: I beg your pardon?

JACQUI: Do you think I'm cuckoo?

TOLLA: No. I do not think you're cuckoo.

JACQUI: Thank you, Tolla. Well, Estelle, it would appear you are wrong. Pass the wine, please.

ESTELLE: Thought you didn't drink.

JACQUI: You've been trying to upset me ever since you arrived. But you're not going to succeed, OK? I've met your sort before.

ESTELLE: And I've met your sort. You bloody snob.

JACQUI: That is the one thing I am not. I most certainly am not a snob.

ESTELLE: Then why do you say you live in the Garden Suburb of Hampstead, when you live in Golders Green?

JACQUI: Now Tolla, what do you do? Have you got a job or anything?

TOLLA: I'm a teacher.

ROSY: A teacher?

They all look at TOLLA.

JACQUI: A teacher?

ESTELLE: In a school?

TOLLA: Yes.

ROSY: My teachers used to call me Rosy bloody Harris.

ESTELLE: What do you teach?

TOLLA: Maths.

ROSY: I failed that. Couldn't get it at any price.

ESTELLE: A teacher.

ROSY: Mind you, I didn't actually pass anything.

JACQUI: Schools aren't what they used to be though.

ROSY: I wish the boys'd hurry up and come home. I'm getting dead worried, me.

JACQUI: Now, Tolla, have you got a fitted kitchen?

TOLLA: I beg your pardon?

ROSY: 'Come and sit up the front, Rosy bloody Harris,' That's what my teacher used to say to me.

ESTELLE: Just so he could have a good shooftie at your knickers, I expect.

ROSY: Do you know, you could have a point there. He was always coming up close, rubbing my back when he was checking my work, seeing if I had a bra on.

TOLLA: We've got wall and base units, I don't know whether it would actually be termed a 'fitted kitchen'. My husband did it himself.

JACQUI: And is he an imparter of knowledge?

TOLLA: No. He just specialises in crime.

JACQUI: We've got a Schreiber. German but terribly good.

ROSY: D'you know what this job is tonight, Tolla?

TOLLA: 'Fraid not.

ROSY: The only link I can suss out is that they might be making dresses for prostitutes to be sold on Nigerian street markets. But I doubt there's an awful lot of bread in that.

TOLLA: They've known each other for years, it could be anything they're working on.

ESTELLE: My Ted's got such a big cake-hole I can't understand why he hasn't spilt the beans. I've known about every one of his other dirty deals. He was in with your old man on exporting 'Band Aid' pirate videos into Africa, wasn't he?

TOLLA: Rather ironic that particular episode.

JACQUI: Of course, kitchens are a great selling point in any house.

ROSY: My Ray fenced some of them videos.

JACQUI *has put her head in her hands and has begun to cry.*

What's the matter, Jacqui love?

ESTELLE: Cuckoo, that's what the bloody matter is.

JACQUI: I just can't bear you talking like that.

ROSY: Don't worry yourself, they'll be indoors soon, and you can stop worrying.

JACQUIE: It's all right for you lot, you'd survive. I wouldn't be able to survive, I know I wouldn't.

ROSY: She's really upset, Estelle.

ESTELLE: Look, I'm sorry, Jacqui, it's just that you were pissing me off with all the crap you were coming out with about the good old honest Jewish tailor. But I'm sorry, I didn't mean to make you cry.

ROSY: There you are. She's said she's sorry. That's nice innit?

JACQUI: Thank you, Estelle. I do appreciate the gesture.

ROSY: There you are. And she appreciates the gesture. That's nice too.

JACQUI: But Manny does make dresses.

ESTELLE: And invest in the child sex slave trade.

ROSY: She's jesting, Jacqui, don't worry yourself.

The phone rings. JACQUI *unsteadily gets to her feet to answer it. She exits.*

JACQUI: 'Highland Retreat'. Mrs Silver speaking.

ROSY: How long have you been married, Tolla?

TOLLA: Three years today.

ESTELLE: Hoping for remission for good behaviour? I tell you what, I must have murdered someone in a previous existence, because being married to Ted is like a bleeding life sentence. Still, I only married him for the money, it's just that he's taking a hell of a long time to die.

ROSY: Ent she wicked, Tolla? But I bet she's having a little joke with us. I bet her and Teddy are a right couple of lovebirds.

ESTELLE: Have you seen him? God, if you'd seen him, you wouldn't put any money on us being a couple of lovebirds.

ROSY: Ray does reckon he farts a lot.

ESTELLE: It's like sleeping with a great fat sack of rotting vegetables. And I'm not just talking smell here, I'm talking sex too.

ROSY: It's sad that, when you suddenly fall out of love.

ESTELLE: I married him because I could have sworn he was about to die. I keep trying to persuade him to take up squash. That'd bloody kill him!

ROSY: Couldn't you try him on a bit of the other. Finish him off that way.

ESTELLE: It has crossed my mind,

darling. But I must say, it crossed it pretty bloody quickly. The thought of doing it with that fat, sweaty walrus more than twice a month is enough to kill me.

ROSY: Walrus? Has he got a tash then?

JACQUI *enters looking pale and distraught.*

TOLLA: What is it, what's the matter, Jacqui?

JACQUI: Something, ladies, has happened. But I want you all to remain calm and composed.

TOLLA: What is it?

JACQUI: That was our solicitor on the phone. We're not to panic. We must remain absolutely calm.

ROSY: What did he say, love? Sit down.

JACQUI: He said not to panic. We are to go to this address in Spain.

JACQUI *raises the piece of paper she is holding.*

Our tickets are at the British Airways desk. We are to go there, taking nothing. We are not to panic but to await further instruction.

ESTELLE: Oh bloody hell. I knew this'd happen. I had a bloody feeling.

ROSY: Oh God, I hope my Ray's all right. He'll crumble under interrogation. He needs me there.

TOLLA: Typical. Typical. I marked the entire fourth year mock exam today. They'll never know.

JACQUI: We're to keep calm.

JACQUI *is slowly beginning to crumble.*

ESTELLE: Actually, prison'll kill him.

JACQUI: My house, my house, my lovely house.

JACQUI *is beginning to scream, getting more and more hysterical.*

ROSY: It's all right, Jacqui, it'll only be till things blow over, then you can come back here.

JACQUI: They're going to take my lovely house from me. I can tell. I can tell. Well I shan't let them. I'm going to chain myself to the front door. I shall, I shall, I shall, I shall, I shall . . .

Because JACQUI *is becoming more and more hysterical,* ROSY *slaps her around the face. Everybody freezes and waits for* JACQUI's *reaction. She immediately changes and becomes hyper-efficient.*

Right, I'll call a cab to take us to the airport.

TOLLA: I wondered why I've been instructed to carry my passport with me at all times.

JACQUI *hurries off to do things.*

ROSY: Me too.

ESTELLE: They must have known something could go wrong on this job.

ROSY: Yeah, they said it was a shit or bust job. I guess this is bust. Or is it shit? I've never really understood that expression.

ESTELLE: Right, well I'm going to powder my nose. I'm going to look stunning as I board that plane. I'm going to have that film star off on holiday air about me.

ESTELLE *exits*

ROSY: I knew I'd end up on the Costa del Crime.

TOLLA: I can't say I'll miss Paradise Estate Comprehensive.

ROSY: It's nice the four of us are together really. I don't think I could have taken this on my own.

TOLLA: I presume they'll be able to send us across some money.

ROSY: They wouldn't see us go short. If we do what they say, they'll look after us.

JACQUI *enters carrying a bag.*

JACQUI: Right, I've thrown a few things

into a bag. I've called the cab, that's on its way, it'll be here any minute.

There is suddenly an earpiercing scream from offstage.

Oh my good Lord, what's that?

TOLLA: Estelle!

ESTELLE enters, looking ashen. She is only wearing one shoe.

ESTELLE: My stiletto went right through its head.

ROSY: What?

ESTELLE: I've just stood on a kitten and my stiletto went right through its head.

JACQUI: Goldie! My little Goldie!

JACQUI runs off stage screaming.

ESTELLE: I can't get my stiletto out of its head, and I'm not going to Spain with one shoe.

The doorbell sounds.

TOLLA: That'll be the cab. I'll let him in.

TOLLA goes to answer the door, as ESTELLE and ROSY throw themselves into each other's arms. We can hear the distant wailing of JACQUI. ROSY goes to rush out to comfort JACQUI, returns, picks up a bottle of booze, and rushes off.

Scene Five

The airport.

JACQUI, ROSY, TOLLA and ESTELLE *are all sitting on bar stools. All wear sunglasses and smoke. JACQUI is clutching her bag. ESTELLE is wearing one stiletto and one desert boot. There is a long silence. ROSY suddenly clasps her hand to her mouth and gasps desperately as she remembers something.*

ROSY: My son! Oh Jesus Christ, I've forgotten about my little boy.

ESTELLE: Who's looking after him now, love?

ROSY: Ray's mum.

ESTELLE: She'll look after him, don't worry.

ROSY: Oh my God, he'll forget me.

ESTELLE: Ray'll bring him over when he comes.

ROSY: My little bubbie.

ESTELLE: Phone up when we get there. It'll be all right.

JACQUI: Least you've still got a bubbie.

ESTELLE: Oh God, you've started her off again.

JACQUI: Shut up, murderer!

ESTELLE: What was it doing in the bloody bathroom, anyway? I thought it was a bath mat, I'm sorry.

JACQUI: Murderer.

ROSY: I'll phone as soon as we get there.

TOLLA: Have you been to Spain before?

ROSY: We went to Estartit for our honeymoon.

TOLLA: Did you have a nice time?

ROSY: I got drunk at the wine-tasting on the first day and spent the rest of the week in bed. Where did you go for your honeymoon?

TOLLA: The Loire Valley.

ESTELLE: I love Wales. It's just the bloody weather that gets me down. Bloody funny smell round here, you noticed it, girls?

JACQUI: She who smelt it dealt it.

The other look at JACQUI.

ESTELLE: It's like being back at Comber Grove Infants. Cheer up, will you, it was only a fucking cat!

JACQUI: I hope one day you suffer like I'm suffering now.

ESTELLE: Look, you'd only have had to leave the thing behind. That wouldn't have been any good, would it? You wouldn't like to think of the thing stuck in the house starving to death,

slowly and painfully, now would you?
No. I reckon this is the best thing that
could possibly have happened. In fact,
I reckon you ought to be thanking me
now.

TOLLA: Maybe when we get to Spain,
we could get another little kitten.

JACQUI: I hate Spanish cats.

ESTELLE: We must be near the kitchens
here. Something stinks.

ROSY: What did you bring in the end,
Jacqui?

JACQUI: What?

ROSY: What have you got in your bag,
Jacqui?

JACQUI: Oh just some bits of jade.

ROSY: What on earth have you bought
that for?

JACQUI: I wouldn't feel right without a
bit of jade round me. I wouldn't.

ESTELLE: Let's have a butchers.

ESTELLE *tries to take the bag.*

JACQUI: Get off you bloody murderer.

ESTELLE: I only want a peak, for God's
sake.

*A struggle ensues between JACQUI
and ESTELLE for the bag. Eventually
ESTELLE is able to pull the bag from
JACQUI. ESTELLE opens it up and is
obviously shocked by what she sees.*

Oh my god, she's brought the fucking
cat. The daft bitch has brought the
fucking cat.

JACQUI: I want to give it a proper burial.

ESTELLE: Twenty-four carat cuckoo.

JACQUI: You understand, don't you
Rosy, you've got children.

ROSY: We can't really take a dead kitten
to Spain with us, darling. It'll cause
suspicion.

ESTELLE: I knew I could smell
something. Get her to put it in the bin,
Rosy.

ROSY: Look, we'll find a nice little boy
and we'll say to him, 'D'you wanna
hold this kitten for a minute?' Then
we'll bugger off.

TOLLA: It's dead.

ROSY: He might not notice. They're not
all that observant, kids.

ESTELLE: Least she's brought my shoe
with it. Thirty-five sovs they were.

*There is an announcement over the
tannoy, calling passengers on the flight
to Spain.*

TOLLA: That's us. Come on, girls.

They stand and prepare to depart.

ESTELLE: Get her to dump that thing or
I'm going to kill her.

ROSY: I will do, don't worry.

ESTELLE *and* TOLLA *exit.*

Jacqui, darling, shall I hold that while
you go and get some duty-frees?

JACQUI *reluctantly hands the bag to
ROSY. JACQUI goes off towards the
duty-frees. ROSY drops the bag and
delves into it. After a struggle she pulls
out ESTELLE's other stiletto from the
kitten's head.*

Scene Six

*On the balcony/terrace of a Spanish
apartment. JACQUI sits on the floor in
her fur coat, looking most depressed.
ESTELLE enters.*

JACQUI: A flatlet above 'Dirty Den's
Burger Paradise' isn't my idea of a
place in the sun.

ESTELLE: Relax Jacqui, for gawd's sake
It's only for a little while, till the men
get here.

JACQUI: How can he do this to me? Me
Nearly secretary of Hampstead Garde
Suburb Drama Society! Fleeing the
country! Well, bang goes my chance o
producing their *Mother Hubbard* this
Christmas.

ROSY *enters.*

ROSY: Here, ent it bloody hot, girls? Ent it bloody hot?

ESTELLE: No wonder there's so much disease out here. You can't move without a fly shooting up your hooter!

ROSY *and* ESTELLE *giggle.*

ROSY: What's the last thing that goes through a fly's mind when it hits the windscreen at a hundred miles an hour? . . . Its arse! D'you get it? Took me weeks to get that one as it goes. When my Ray told me, I laughed, mind. I didn't know what he was going on about. But I laughed. You know, like you do. You didn't get it, did you, Jacqui?

JACQUI: Bang goes my chance of winning the street game in the *Evening Standard.* I only needed two more ticks and I'd have won Bond Street.

ROSY: Bloody glad to see they sell decent food out here! All that fruit don't half give you the trots! Here, it's really nice out here, ent it?

TOLLA *enters.*

TOLLA: There are several young men with Union-Jack shorts being sick into the swimming pool.

ESTELLE: Like a Bounty advert.

JACQUI: Oh my God, this is like some weird nightmare.

ROSY: Least there's plenty to do out here, Jac.

JACQUI: Dodgems and discos! What has it all come to?

ROSY: Listen! I can hear someone singing. 'Here we go! Here we go! Here we go!' It's funny really but somehow one doesn't feel quite so homesick when one hears that, does one?

TOLLA: Just sick.

ESTELLE: Look, let's have a nice cup of Rosy, yeh?

ROSY: Rosy . . . Rosy Lee . . . me!

ESTELLE: Then we'll have a swill and hit the town. Let's face it, there's bugger-all we can do about anything now. Just wait! I'll put the kettle on.

ESTELLE *goes inside. Silence.*

ROSY: Don't you like dodgems then, Jac love? I love them, me.

ESTELLE *returns.*

ESTELLE: No tea.

ROSY (*sings*): 'If you're sitting at home or relaxing
Or you're working in a noisy factory
Just set yourself free
When the clock strikes three
Cos everything stops for tea!'
I sing that in the salon.

ESTELLE: That doesn't surprise me.

ROSY: Don't it? It surprises the clients.

TOLLA: Has anybody got any money?

ROSY: Me and Ray have got some premium bonds my grandad left us. But we're not going to touch 'em till we've won something. Cos I want to go into an estate agents, choose a home, and put the money in cash down on his desk, just to see his face.

TOLLA: Has anyone got any money, here and now?

ROSY: 'How much is that one,' I'm gonna say. 'One hundred and fifty thousand? That's fine!' And I'm gonna plonk the whole lot on his desk, in fivers, without ever inquiring as to if they've got double glazing!

ESTELLE: I've got about two quid.

TOLLA: Jacqui?

JACQUI: I don't carry money.

ROSY: Like the Queen!

JACQUI: Thank you, Rosy.

TOLLA: Have you got any money on you, Rosy!

ROSY: No, I've just got my travel card. There's four days left before it expires.

TOLLA: Well unless we get some bread,

we're going to expire. There's nothing to eat in the flat.

JACQUI: And the beds are as hard as rock. Last night was the most unpleasant night of my life. I didn't sleep a wink.

ROSY: You was snoring away like a good 'un.

JACQUI *glares at* ROSY.

Sorry!

ESTELLE: I tell you what, I enjoyed last night. I'd got me own little bed, me own little space. I didn't have to put up with a great white arse shoving me into the Teasmade.

ROSY: D'you get the tap end?

ESTELLE: Eh?

ROSY: Well that might not be the cleanest bath I've ever seen . . .

JACQUI: It's alive!

ROSY: But I must admit that's the first time I've laid down in a bath for years. I'm normally wedged up the end in between Ray's knees and the mixer tap. 'Oh shut up babes, I'm only swilling my bollocks!'

TOLLA: Why've you got your coat on, Jacqui?

JACQUI: Because I'm not staying! As soon as the men arrive I am insisting on being deported.

TOLLA: Well I'm going to go into town and find a bank. See if I can get some money.

ESTELLE: You be careful out there, Tolla.

ROSY: You sounded like *Hill Street Blues*.

JACQUI: Trying to find the apartment last night, I felt my life was in serious danger on several occasions.

ROSY: I thought they were a bit of a laugh, them lads from Bolton.

JACQUI: They were the lowest form of life to have ever crawled out from under a stone.

ESTELLE: That one who was trying to get us to join in that game with the Bloody Marys and tampons is in insurance.

TOLLA: Well thank God my house has never burned down! Look, I'll see you later on, girls.

ROSY: Yeah.

ESTELLE: Terrah.

TOLLA *goes.*

Maybe I should have gone with her.

ROSY: She'll be all right. When that guy started to give her a bit of the verbal last night, she told him she was Brazilian and he ended up buying her a drink! She's a survivor, our Tolla.

JACQUI: And I'm the Titanic, I suppose.

ROSY: We done *Midsummer Night's Dream* for our CSE.

ESTELLE: Look at it as a holiday, Jac love.

JACQUI: The thing about Ilford . . . you're born, you get married, and you die. None of this!

ESTELLE: Take your coat off and get a bit of sun on you.

JACQUI: The minute it's off my back it'll be pawned for paella.

ESTELLE: Fortunately they don't get a lot of call for that round here.

ROSY: What do we do if they've got put away?

ESTELLE: Don't worry, Rosy darling. They'll sort something out.

JACQUI: Never mind about her, what about me? It's taken me years to reach the position I've reached today . . . or rather yesterday . . . what do I do at my age?

ESTELLE: You get up off your arse and stop being so bloody pathetic.

JACQUI: I'm not used to this sort of existence. Stop shouting at me!

ESTELLE: I'm not shouting at you, dear.

JACQUI: Don't 'dear' me. I am not your 'dear'.

ESTELLE: Oh gawd. I'm going to get something to drink.

She goes. Silence. JACQUI sits looking totally morose. ROSY tries to think of something to say. She opens her mouth but nothing comes out. This happens several times until eventually:

ROSY: Do you bite your nails? I know I shouldn't but I do! Don't ask me why. Well, you can if you want to, but I wouldn't know what to answer! I just . . . do it! 'I'll dip your fingers in mustard, if you carry on,' my Ray's always saying to me. He did once. Funny thing is, I quite like mustard. Well, I suppose it's not that funny. Anyway. Do you realise it's about this time yesterday I was meeting you. 'Hello I'm Rosy.' 'Hello I'm Jacqui.' And here we are! Abroad! Well, blow me down. Twenty-four hours on and here we are overlooking . . .

She looks out.

. . . the 'Star of Bombay India Restaurant'! Here, that's clever innit, they've even got Indian restaurants out here, in case anyone's feeling homesick! That's nice.

Silence.

You see when a fly hits the windscreen of a car, it gets all squashed up, and supposing its nose hits the windscreen first . . . do flies have noses? I suppose they must really, else how do they smell? Yeah I know, awful! Anyway where was I? Oh yeah, so a fly's nose hits the windscreen, and wham! the rest of it follows, so . . . the last . . .

ESTELLE enters with a bottle of champagne.

Estelle! Thank God you're back, I was beginning to feel like Ronnie Corbett.

ESTELLE: Champagne!

ROSY: You haven't got any money!

Where did you get it from, you genius.

ESTELLE: I had to give the barman the longest sob-story you have ever heard. About how my mother died when I was three, and how I was brought up by a wicked stepfather who used to beat and abuse me, and tie me in a sack, and make me sleep in the fish pond with just my head sticking out of the water, and how I have only just managed to escape his wicked ways and fled to Spain in an attempt to start a new life.

ROSY: And he gave you the champagne?

ESTELLE: No, then I showed him my tits and that seemed to do the trick. Men are funny creatures.

ESTELLE opens the champagne and they drink from the bottle. JACQUI is lying prostrate on the floor, crying.

Have you been singing to her again?

ROSY: I was trying to cheer her up.

TOLLA enters.

TOLLA: Right girls, prepare yourselves for a shock!

ROSY: That was just like a teacher. Well done Tolla . . . Miss.

TOLLA: Imagine the worst . . .

ESTELLE: They've gone down, haven't they? I can tell by her voice, they've got put away.

TOLLA: On discovering all my credit cards had been stopped, I telephoned England to discover that last night was the completion date on all our houses. They have been sold . . . lock, stock and barrel. There was no 'big job'. Well, the only job there was, was to get us out of the way. They have sold everything they owned and bought this bar in Australia! They've gone there to start a new life . . . without us! They must have been scheming this for months.

ROSY: My Ray?

TOLLA: All four of them.

ROSY: I don't believe it! My Ray wouldn't do that to me.

ESTELLE: Last year's model. Story of my bloody life! They get all the bread, we get the crumbs . . . this poxy little Spanish apartment.

TOLLA: Not quite. I've just had a chat with Dirty Den downstairs. It appears the men have only rented this, and only paid a deposit. We have to find the balance on our departure . . . next Tuesday!

ROSY: I suppose his mother's got little Ray.

JACQUI has stood up and has begun to intone . . . gently at first but gradually increasing in volume . . .

JACQUI: Fuck. Fuck. Fuck. Fuck. Fuck. Fuck. Fuck.

She continues as she attempts to climb over the terrace wall and throw herself off. The others, on realising this, grab hold of her and pin her down to prevent this action.

ROSY: Oh my gawd! Thursdays!

The lights fade down.

Scene Seven

A bar. Later that night. The four women sit around a table on which is a bottle of coke with four straws.

ESTELLE: Fuck them!

She takes a sip of the coke and passes it on.

TOLLA: Fuck them!

She takes a sip of the coke and passes it on.

ROSY: Fuck them!

She takes a sip of the coke and passes it on.

JACQUI: Fuck them!

She takes a sip of the coke and passes it on.

ESTELLE: What we need is a strategy.

TOLLA: We've got to get some money by Tuesday.

ROSY: You all right, Jacqui?

JACQUI: Much better, thank you.

ROSY: Tell you what, even if you'd have managed to throw yourself off, your fall would have been broken by all them chip wrappers.

JACQUI: It was just the shock.

ESTELLE: You'll be all right, Jacqui. We'll look after you.

JACQUI: Yes. I feel that. I feel that and I thank you.

ESTELLE: Better to have lost the money and the men, than to have lost the money and kept the men.

JACQUI: The Lord giveth and the Lord taketh away.

ESTELLE: Yeah but he aint half keen on the taking away.

TOLLA: We've got to do something.

ROSY: I can't believe my Ray left me with nothing.

TOLLA: Stopping the credit cards!

ESTELLE: Wicked innit?

ROSY: Once I get enough money, I'm going back to rescue my baby from his mother! She's a monster. She's only teeth and hair short of being locked up.

ESTELLE: I tell you what, even though I shall miss his money, I shall hardly miss his sparkling wit and intelligence. And I certainly shan't miss his penis. Waving that great thing about going, 'Oh go on, I'd do it if you had one.'

TOLLA: They don't know what it's like for a woman!

JACQUI: I tell you what, I expect I'll miss Wogan more than I'll miss sex.

ESTELLE: Oh I don't mind sex, it's just Ted I can't stand.

JACQUI: I've never really enjoyed sex. Someone once said that was my problem.

ESTELLE: The only sex problems women have are men.

ROSY: I've always enjoyed sex. That's been my problem.

JACQUI: All sex has ever meant to me is another sheet to wash.

TOLLA: I'm looking forward to doing my own washing, when I want to! And not doing it when I don't!

ESTELLE: Now, we gotta plan some sort of strategy.

JACQUI (*looking around*): Christ, there are some animals in here!

ESTELLE: We could ponce food and drink off of these animals for a little while . . . but we need rent money.

TOLLA: Let's do something on our own.

ESTELLE: Well, I could return to the oldest profession in the world.

JACQUI: And where are you going to get a job teaching?

TOLLA: That's not a bad idea. I should be able to get some sort of teaching. With all the Brits here, there must be some schools for their kids.

ROSY: I could do the odd Barnet. Yeah, I know, the very odd Barnet!

ESTELLE: I say as soon as we've got enough dosh we plonk you on the first plane back to Blighty so's you can sort out little Ray.

TOLLA: Definitely. Even before we pay off Dirty Den.

JACQUI: What do I do when I get back to England? I'm sorry to appear so self-pitying, Estelle. I am sorry. It's just that I feel so damned unprepared. I can't do anything. I'm so useless. I can't even have children.

There is a pause while the three look at JACQUI. *They are not quite sure how to respond.* ROSY *suddenly gives her a big hug.*

ROSY: It's all right, Jacs. Don't worry, babes. We've all got a lot of adjusting to do.

JACQUI: I suppose I shouldn't really be surprised. I mean, I'm not really sure what Manny and I had in the beginning but I'm sure we haven't got anything left.

ESTELLE: Would you take Ray back, Rosy?

ROSY: I thought we had something special, me and Ray. But no, I wouldn't take him back. Not now. Would you take Ted back?

ESTELLE: Yes. Then I'd get insurance and kill the bastard.

JACQUI: There's a terrible smell of vomit in here.

TOLLA: There's someone being sick over there.

JACQUI: Do you think our men behave like this when they're on their own?

ESTELLE: God help Austra-fucking-lasia!

Scene Eight

In gaol in Spain. JACQUI, ESTELLE *and* TOLLA *lie underneath regulation prison blankets.*

JACQUI: Married to a man with an executive 'walk-about' phone, and here I am, wallowing in the depths of the Third World's penal system.

TOLLA: They are in the EEC.

ESTELLE: That's probably why we got a butter mountain. The bread that screw gave us this morning was like polystyrene!

TOLLA: What do you mean?

ESTELLE: Well the Spanish obviously never use it and it's building up like a mountain!

JACQUI: I feel so pure!

ESTELLE: Never mind, ay?

JACQUI: Somehow, here we are, paying our debt to the system! We didn't pay our rent money, so they put us in the cooler as a penance.

TOLLA: I'm glad we got Rosy back home!

JACQUI: Yes, she'll be with her Little Ray now. I bet he's lovely, her Little Ray.

ESTELLE: Well he's gotta be nicer than Big Ray.

JACQUI: You know, in some ways I can understand what Manny did to me. I probably wasn't the sort of wife he wanted.

ESTELLE: Don't blame yourself cos he's a turd, darling.

JACQUI: But I can't really understand why Ray abandoned Rosy.

ESTELLE: He was just the same as the others. A bit thinner, but still a tin of maggots.

TOLLA: My husband's going to come crawling back to me! I know he will. I'm going to enjoy being really friendly and smiling, as I carry on with my life. He's got a history of wanting 'something more'. And when he's bored with it, it's the slow slime back to old Tolla. Well this time old Tolla's not having him back.

ESTELLE: Good for you, girl.

TOLLA: He's always been able to push me about physically but he's never known what's gone on inside my head. I've always won, up there. While he's been pawing me, inside my head I'm being stroked and loved by the finest, most handsome and refined gentleman in the world.

ESTELLE: Oh yeah, whenever Ted's on the job I'm always thinking of Sylvester Stallone too.

TOLLA: I shut my eyes and think of . . . Nigeria.

ESTELLE: Mind you, old Ted's hardly the Italian stallion to look at. More like the cockney donkey, in fact.

TOLLA: Even in here, if we shut our eyes and breathe in, we can be in the most wonderful summer meadow.

JACQUI: Yes. It's just that there's a terrible smell of urine.

ESTELLE: Not as clean as our English nicks, see. They've obviously no pride.

JACQUI: What can you expect from a country that is so cruel to animals?

TOLLA: Yet even in here, I feel somehow . . . elated.

JACQUI: I feel somehow constipated.

ESTELLE: Yeah, they call it Spanish tummy.

TOLLA: I'm not going back!

ESTELLE: What d'you mean?

TOLLA: I know I should feel at an all-time low now, but in many ways I feel nothing but a sense of relief. I mean, what's the point in going back? I'll be starting off from scratch back home, I might as well start off from scratch over here.

ESTELLE: My trouble is, what does an ageing massage parlour assistant do? I guess it's too late to go into politics or medicine. All that's left for me is to search for the masseurs' graveyard.

JACQUI: I always wanted to be a doctor.

ESTELLE: Don't tell me, you never had the patience.

JACQUI: Never had the brains. Mind you, I don't think Ilford is the natural breeding ground for the profession.

ESTELLE: It's the breeding ground for a few things though. One of the girls did a job there and got well dosed. But apparently that's the only thing ever to have come out of Ilford.

They laugh. ESTELLE *stands and calls out to the prison warden.*

ESTELLE: Oi, what about some more polystyrene down here! It's not asking a lot really, is it? I mean, if it wasn't for us Brits, this place would still be a backward little fishing village, and you'd be going off to work on a donkey, so I reckon a little bit of grub would be a symbol of your gratitude.

Scene Nine.

A new apartment in Spain. JACQUI *sits in a chair, looking at her watch.* TOLLA *enters.*

JACQUI: She'll be nearly home by now.

TOLLA: Mmm?

JACQUI: Estelle. She should be nearly home by now. It's so good you got the job. Teaching English as a foreign language. You're so clever, Tolla.

TOLLA: You'll be all right here on your own today?

JACQUI: Of course. What I'm going to do is see if I can find some material because I'm going to start making you some curtains. It's such a nice apartment. Do all teachers get one then?

TOLLA: No. It's just that the headmistress knows lots and lots of places you can rent a little off the main tourist routes.

JACQUI: It's really nice and Spanishy, this area. You sure you don't mind me stopping on for a bit?

TOLLA: Of course not. You stop on as long as you like, Jacqui. Don't forget though if you do ever want to go back home, you've only to ask for the flight money, you know.

JACQUI: Oh I know. Thanks. It's just that I don't really have anything to go back to. You know. I could go back and stop with my sister, I suppose, but I don't really fancy that. Besides, out here, it's like getting another chance. It's like starting all over again. I made a bit of a muck up, the first time.

TOLLA: Jacqui, I'm not sure yet, but there's a possibility that they're looking for a classroom assistant in the kindergarten. I wondered, if maybe I had a word with the head, whether you'd like to come in and meet her, and see if you think the job would suit you.

JACQUI: Me?

TOLLA: Yes.

JACQUI: Really? Do you mean it? Me? A classroom assistant? Me?

TOLLA: I'll see if I can have a word.

JACQUI: Oh Tolla!

The door opens. It is ESTELLE.

ESTELLE: Right get the kettle on, I'm coughing feathers here.

TOLLA: Estelle!

JACQUI: What are you doing back?

ESTELLE: Well, I was about to board the plane, when I bumped into an old friend of mine.

In walks ROSY.

JACQUI: Rosy!

TOLLA: Rosy!

JACQUI: It's Rosy!

ESTELLE: Everything's coming up Rosy!

ROSY: Hi girls! I've just put little Ray down on one of the beds. He fell asleep in the taxi coming here. Nice gaff, isn't it?

JACQUI: What are you doing back, Rosy?

ROSY: Well I thought you'd still be in prison. I'd come to get you out. Cos I'd heard, in these foreign gaols, they keep you locked up for months, with no food or nothing, then they make you go and fight the bulls, with no training, or nothing.

JACQUI: I must go and see little Ray. I love him already.

JACQUI *hurries off.*

ROSY: How's Jacqui been?

TOLLA: Quite painless. Since we persuaded her to take those electrodes from behind her ears, she's been wonderful. You heard I got a job at the International School?

ROSY: Yeah, Estelle told me. That's really something.

JACQUI *comes back in.*

JACQUI: You're right, Rosy. He's so cuddly. And he has got fat legs.

TOLLA: The monster wasn't any trouble then?

ROSY: I didn't give her any bloody choice, I can tell you.

ESTELLE: She was in and out quicker than Ted.

ROSY: I whisked him straight out and was on my way round to my brother's in the Old Father Red-Cap when I bumped into Finger 'The Bank' Davidson and Smudge 'The Building Society' McGuire. Anyway it turns out they've got a little bar, a couple of miles along the coast from here and they're looking for a couple of young dollies to run it for them . . . cos there's no point in them coming back now Spain have agreed an extradition treaty with Britain.

ESTELLE: And me and Rosy are gonna be them young dollies!

ROSY: It's lucky I bumped into you at the airport!

TOLLA: That's great news.

ESTELLE: We are going to have the most thriving little bar for miles. Bacon and egg of a morning, pie and mash of a dinner-time.

ROSY: Marmite sarnies for tea . . .

ESTELLE: And we're planning on calling it something typically Spanish.

ROSY: Por Favor, we was thinking of. You know, like the song. 'España Por Favor'. It's so lucky I saw you at the airport.

ESTELLE: It is, or you wouldn't have known where to come.

ROSY: That's true. This is better than Dirty Den's innit?

JACQUI: This is home!

The lights fade down to blackout.

.